"I am convinced that the application of  *Making Waves* will change lives. My ch read the book, you will become convinc 'destined to be people who make wave family, friends, communities, and worl
—BILL THRALL, leadership i.

coauthor of *TrueFaced*

"Full of grace and truth aptly describes Doug Nuenke's excellent book. Drawing from lessons learned in his own life, he gently challenges and shows us how to be instruments of grace to those we encounter in our everyday lives. All who desire to be useful in kingdom work will profit from this book."
—JERRY BRIDGES, author of *Respectable Sins*, *The Pursuit of Holiness*, and *Trusting God*

"Doug Nuenke weaves biblical teaching, personal experience, and practical advice into a guidebook for Christian living."
—LEITH ANDERSON, president, National Association of Evangelicals, Washington, DC; pastor, Wooddale Church, Eden Prairie, Minnesota

"Have you come face-to-face with your black-hearted behavior or, on the flip side, the pride of how wonderful you are, only to realize the loneliness of a life without meaning or purpose? There is only one fix: a tsunami, a wave of grace, only found in Christ. In Doug's book *Making Waves*, we are given a road map to experience this 'grace wave' and then the keys to how we can pass it on. Waves are transforming! Let Doug's book guide you into the most wonderful transformation ever. Ride the wave!"
—TIMOTHY J. McKIBBEN, founding managing partner, Anchor Capital Partners

"In modern times, it's never been more important to proclaim the gospel of Jesus Christ. That is exactly what *Making Waves* accomplishes. For too long, followers of Jesus have been complacent. In the gospels, we see that Jesus was in the business of making waves right up to the Cross. If we are to be authentic, we must put aside our fears and start doing things the way Jesus did. That's what this book is all about, and I strongly endorse it."
—MIKE TIMMIS, chairman, Prison Fellowship; business owner and CEO

"Doug Nuenke is passionate about reaching others with the good news of Christ. In *Making Waves*, he shares about lessons learned from many years in ministry as well as practical guidance to help you carry out the Great Commission. He not only writes well, he lives well. An authentic book by an authentic man."

—DR. JOE WHITE, president, Kanakuk Kamps

"Many of us know about being emptied, but it's another thing to go through the painful process of heaving to trust in God fully in a life that demands His mercies. Doug Nuenke knows that through truth and through experience. As Christians grow through the process, they will find this a comforting read."

—TOMMY NELSON, senior pastor,
Denton Bible Church, Denton, Texas

"Doug Nuenke is a man of great faithfulness and integrity. In his wonderful book *Making Waves*, he does a great job of helping us understand all that Christ wants us to be and do. *Making Waves* will at times convict you and challenge you as well as touch you with God's love and grace. Doug helps us understand the Christian life with its joys and sorrows, failures and opportunities. As sent ones, we can go into the world filled with God's Word, grace, and power. This is a great read!"

—JIM DIXON, DMin, founding and senior pastor,
Cherry Hills Community Church, Highlands Ranch, Colorado;
author of *Vice and Virtue* and *Last Things Revealed*

"The students with whom I work want to make a difference in the world. Doug Nuenke takes a fresh look at how ordinary people can become extraordinary world changers as they pursue a life transformed and used by Jesus. *Making Waves* is both practical and compelling."

—STEPHEN A. HAYNER, PhD, president,
Columbia Theological Seminary

"Doug reminds us that God has a plan that includes all of us: whole or broken; the extraordinary, the ordinary, and the less than ordinary. He challenges us to find where we fit and to ask ourselves if we are open to letting God use us where we are."

—RONALD CAMERON, chairman, Mountaire Corporation

"This is a winsome work, full of good humor and graceful applications to real life. Read it and be inspired to make waves of grace right where you are!"

—DR. RUTH HALEY BARTON, founder, Transforming Center; author of *Sacred Rhythms: Arranging Our Lives for Spiritual Transformation*

"With engaging personal narrative, Doug Nuenke shows how the time-honored practice of disciplemaking unfolds beyond mere programs into breathtaking dimensions. This vision for missional living will give fresh hope for how God works in and through our lives. Doug captures our hearts with energizing and hopeful conviction, showing how God uses our deepest longings and unexpected experiences to build His kingdom."

—DON J. PAYNE, PhD, associate dean/assistant professor of theology and ministry, Denver Seminary

"*Making Waves* is the life story and message of a man who has been walking with Jesus and impacting others for decades. Read it, absorb it, let it flow down into your spiritual bloodstream to help shape your life story and message too!"

—DR. STEVE SHADRACH, president, The BodyBuilders; director of mobilization, U.S. Center for World Mission

"There is incredible power in the realization that our lives have significance—not just in the idea that God has an individual purpose for each of us but in the startling truth that He invites each of us to participate in His grand purpose for all of human history. *Making Waves*, written with the clarity and wisdom of someone who lives with that compelling sense of purpose, will lead you into a wonderful awareness that each and every day of your life matters because God is using you to accomplish His eternal purpose: that all people worship Him alone."

—DR. MARK YOUNG, president, Denver Seminary

"This inspirational book is filled with insight to help clarify your calling and define your destiny through your daily decisions. On every page, Doug authentically shows how to generate 'waves of grace' that will profoundly impact the everyday person."

—JUNE HUNT, CEO and CSO (Chief Servant Officer), Hope for the Heart; author of *Hope for Your Heart: Finding Strength in Life's Storms*

"I know of no one better than Doug Nuenke to speak about the waves of God's grace. Doug is a grace-filled man—that is, he is one who has received God's grace in his own life and knows how to lead others to receive this grace as well. Sharing openly and honestly from his own experiences of brokenness and need, Doug lays out how God's grace has transformed and is transforming his own life. He then shows us how we can both receive this grace and lead others to it. Indeed, this book could end as Paul's letters, 'Grace be with you.' As a pastor who desires to lead a church grounded in and transformed by grace, I heartily commend this book!"

—REVEREND WILLIAM VOGLER, pastor, Grace Evangelical Presbyterian Church, Lawrence, Kansas; moderator of the 27th General Assembly of the Evangelical Presbyterian Church

"There's a big difference between making a splash and making waves. Doug Nuenke's book isn't about calling attention to yourself but rather doing something way more important and lasting: letting others experience the influence of Jesus. That's an experience you (and they) don't want to miss."

—MARSHALL SHELLEY, editor, *Leadership*, www.christianitytoday.com

"In *Making Waves*, Doug shares his lifetime journey of loving people and introducing them to Jesus of Nazareth. He not only gives us great practical advice but also reveals the heart of a discipler and the historic legacy of The Navigators."

—MARK L. EARLEY, president, Prison Fellowship, USA

DOUG NUENKE

MAKING
WAVES

*Being an Influence for Jesus
in Everyday Life*

NavPress is the publishing ministry of The Navigators, an international Christian organization and leader in personal spiritual development. NavPress is committed to helping people grow spiritually and enjoy lives of meaning and hope through personal and group resources that are biblically rooted, culturally relevant, and highly practical.

For a free catalog go to www.NavPress.com or call 1.800.366.7788 in the United States or 1.800.839.4769 in Canada.

ISBN-13: 978-1-61747-920-5

Cover design by Arvid Wallen
Cover photo by Galyna Andrushko, Shutterstock

Some of the anecdotal illustrations in this book are true to life and are included with the permission of the persons involved. All other illustrations are composites of real situations, and any resemblance to people living or dead is coincidental.

Unless otherwise identified, all Scripture quotations in this publication are taken from the *Holy Bible, New International Version*® (NIV®). Copyright © 1973, 1978, 1984 by Biblica, used by permission of Zondervan. All rights reserved. Other versions used include: the *Holy Bible*, New Living Translation (NLT), copyright © 1996. Used by permission of Tyndale House Publishers, Inc., Wheaton, Illinois 60189. All rights reserved; the *Holy Bible*, New Living Translation (NLTSE), copyright © 1996, 2004. Used by permission of Tyndale House Publishers, Inc., Wheaton, Illinois 60189. All rights reserved; *THE MESSAGE* (MSG). Copyright © 1993, 1994, 1995, 1996, 2000, 2001, 2002. Used by permission of NavPress Publishing Group; The Holy Bible, English Standard Version (ESV), copyright © 2001 by Crossway Bibles, a division of Good News Publishers. Used by permission. All rights reserved.

Nuenke, Doug, 1958-
  Making waves : being an influence for Jesus in everyday life / Doug Nuenke.
    p. cm.
  Includes bibliographical references.
  ISBN 978-1-61747-920-5
  1. Influence (Psychology)--Religious aspects--Christianity. 2. Christian life. I. Title.
  BV4597.53.I52N84 2011
  248.4--dc23
                              2011034258

Printed in the United States of America

1 2 3 4 5 6 7 8 / 17 16 15 14 13 12 11

To my wife, Pam,

I can't imagine a better partner in making waves.

We've spent our years together investing in the lives of our

family and others, with the hope that they would be followers

of Christ and also become wavemakers. And by God's grace,

so many have. I look forward to the years to come as we continue

to serve Jesus, each other, and those God brings across our paths.

This book is also dedicated to everyday people: men and women

working jobs, raising families, living in cities and communities—

people who desire to follow Jesus in the midst of everyday

life and want to help others do the same.

CONTENTS

ACKNOWLEDGMENTS

I WOULD LIKE to express deep appreciation to the people who have had a godly influence in my life—and to a large degree, who have written this book by writing on my life's parchment. There are so many, and my life is richer for the mark you have left.

Special thanks to:

Mom and Dad for forming the values of loving others and diligence into my life.

My kids: Beth Ann, Lauren, and Will, who have patiently endured years of busy activity, a house filled with people, and much travel—I constantly learn from you.

Craig McElvain, who taught me how to walk with Jesus as a college student.

Richard Beach, my lifelong mentor, who modeled a passion for telling others about Christ.

Will Cunningham, Bob Beltz, Mike Jordahl, and Fred Wevodau, who model the spiritual life, creativity, a hunger for the Word, humility, and a heart for people.

Cary, Susan, Fish, Steve, Anne, Tom, Dana, Kevin, Katie, Brian, and Debbie, who walk with me in life, encouraging, advising, celebrating, and mourning all of life's ups and downs—you help keep me God-focused and following in the steps of Jesus.

The Navigators National Leadership team, especially Mike Miller, for their encouragement to write this book.

Becky Neumann for helping me keep this project going and in my schedule.

Katherine Dinsdale for your many hours, incredible input, editing, and guidance during the first drafts.

Brian Thomasson for your helpful editing and architecting to help me bring this message to life.

YOU, TOO, CAN MAKE SOME WAVES!

The place God calls you to is the place where your deep gladness and the world's deep hunger meet.

— FREDERICK BUECHNER

HAVE YOU EVER found yourself perplexed by life, wondering if your days are counting for anything? Have you ever struggled through a whiny season of continual doubts? Perhaps at such times you've asked yourself questions like:

Is it worth finishing what I've started?

What direction should I head now?

Do my footprints on this planet really make a difference?

A number of times in my life I have languished in that same boat, asking those same tired questions. Early in my freshman year of college I was directionless and drifting, but God was not far off. I was drawn into a new and genuine faith through the influence of some other freshmen who had a real and winsome walk with Jesus. Learning that God had a purpose for my life was one of the first promises I was taught as a new believer. Psalm 139:13-14 showed me God's individual intent and activity in my existence:

For you created my inmost being;
*   you knit me together in my mother's womb.*
I praise you because I am fearfully and wonderfully made;
*   your works are wonderful,*
*   I know that full well.*

Jeremiah 29:11 further cemented my hope in God's purposeful design and plan for me: "'For I know the plans I have for you,' declares the Lord, 'plans to prosper you and not to harm you, plans to give you hope and a future.'"

All of us remember those heady days of discovery as new believers, finding the gold of God's promises for the first time. But all of us also endure times when we live with a huge gap between those truths and our outlook on life. We wonder how to *experience* and join God in these promises. We know God does not want us drifting aimlessly, questioning the influence He intends us to have in this world. We understand He has designed each of us with a purpose, and He has a contribution in mind for each of us to make. The problem is living out what we profess and believe.

As I travel around the country and the world, I meet many believers struggling and questioning along the same lines. Many worry they are coming up short spiritually and are lacking in community. Often they are questioning whether they are making a dent in our lost, hope-hungry world. Over the last two decades, doubt has grown in the western church concerning the effectiveness of the body of Christ in reaching the current and next generation of Americans. Many Christian authors have sought to point this out and bring clarity and correction to our mission and purpose as the church.[1] There is a desperate need for every believer to clarify the kind of influence he or she can have in our hurting world. Sadly though, many believers have come to mistakenly believe that the real ministry of Christ is for professional ministers and mythic spiritual heroes like Billy Graham or Andy Stanley. While the efforts of professional spiritual leaders should not be discounted, the greatest influence in the world today could be felt by the accumulated influence of everyday people living out the kingdom life as God intended.

Observers of the culture and observers of the western church are also sending up warnings regarding the lack of community among believers and the steadily diminishing influence of the church in our society. The change of cultural landscape, along with eroded trust in the church, has impacted our ability to engage purposefully in our world today. Pam and I have been a part of great local churches, but we all see that at times church culture can become out of step in understanding nonbelieving people today. And perhaps it is even worse that the watching world is confused when it looks at those who call themselves Christians living by the same standards as they do.

Authors Hirsch and Frost see a lack of life integrity as the culprit and agree that believers too often live with a gap between belief and everyday life. This credibility gap will only be overcome with a more "whole-of-life spirituality."[2] The emerging generation is less drawn to propositions alone. They long to see authentic faith that impacts life. Each of us needs the courage and know-how to step up and be that example by the grace of God.

In his book *LeadershipNext*, Eddie Gibbs asserts that the greatest concern for followers of Christ should not be how to get people to come to church but how best to take the church into the world.[3] For this to work, though, we need the church to be a place of transformation, not just activity. In a startling disclosure in 2004, Bill Hybels and the leadership of Willow Creek Community Church acknowledged that in the thirty years Willow Creek had existed, the church had not accomplished one of the chief goals they had set out to accomplish: the transformation of the lives of their people. Their "Reveal" study surveyed the congregation and found that the assumption of the church's leaders that participation in church activity would lead to spiritual growth was wrong. In fact, survey results seemed to indicate that participation in church activities had very little correlation to individuals' spiritual growth in loving God and loving others.[4]

Other perhaps less surprising research shows that men and women in their twenties are disconnected from many of the expressions of today's church. With these findings, the prospects of twenty- and thirtysomethings finding a community where they can grow in faith and live out their kingdom destiny look dim. Certainly our world and particularly many younger men and women need renewed hope that they can have an influence and make a contribution for the sake of Christ.

All of us need to understand that we can participate in making waves of grace cascade into a spiritually thirsty world.

A PERFECT STORM OF GRACE

Despite the seeming constant gap between truth and practice in our lives, God is faithful. He is constantly holding out opportunities for us to reconnect and recalibrate.

Let's fast-forward to my sophomore year of college. It was a life-altering year. I began to discover who I was designed to be and the purpose for which God had made me. Through the influence of some students who were pursuing and learning from Jesus, I discovered my own destiny. These students were influenced by some ideas seen in the life and ministry of Jesus. These ideas were also trumpeted during those years by an organization called The Navigators. During that year I read a book called *Disciples Are Made, Not Born*, another book called *The Master Plan of Evangelism*, and heard a recording of the founder of The Navigators, Dawson Trotman, giving his historic message, "Born to Reproduce." These influences were a personal perfect storm that totally reconfigured the landscape of my life.

To top off the year, on a spring break trip with a mentor named Bob, God spoke with clarity and in an uncanny way to give me a glimpse of His purpose for my life. I was at Newport Beach in Southern

California, spending time reading my Bible and listening to God. As I lay on a beach blanket, paging through the book of Genesis, I came upon these words, a promise given to Abraham, the father of the people of Israel:

> *I will surely bless you and make your descendants as numerous as the stars in the sky and as the sand on the seashore. Your descendants will take possession of the cities of their enemies, and through your offspring all nations on earth will be blessed, because you have obeyed me.* (Genesis 22:17-18)

I also understood that the Bible tells us that every person who puts his or her faith in Christ becomes a spiritual descendant of Abraham: "And now that you belong to Christ, you are the true children of Abraham. You are his heirs, and now all the promises God gave to him belong to you" (Galatians 3:29, NLT). So the promise I read on that beach was an astonishing revelation to me. With billions of particles of sand all around me, sticking to my blanket and to my body, the metaphor in God's promise could not have been more clear! My life could be blessed by God in such a way that people, as many as the grains of sand on that beach, would be touched by God's goodness through my life. Now that's something worth living for!

Another passage of Scripture that stands at the center of what grabbed my heart that year was 2 Timothy 2:1-2: "You then, my son, be strong in the grace that is in Christ Jesus. And the things you have heard me say in the presence of many witnesses entrust to reliable men who will also be qualified to teach others."

The apostle Paul encourages his son in the faith, Timothy, to grab hold of two foundational life principles. First, *life* is fully experienced through the grace of God, the gift of God that is found in Jesus Christ. Second, those of us who have embraced and had our lives marked by God's grace are to pass along the knowledge and reality of

Christ to others through waves of grace—His reverberating influence through us.

Through people impacted by the grace and goodness of God, a ripple of grace begins which impacts all those around. And through family members and friends affected by Jesus Christ, an unstoppable wave of gracious influence continues out into other families and communities, even crossing oceans and national boundaries.

Hear me clearly: Our identity and purpose as those created by God is for us to be conduits of this grace to others. We were destined to be people who make waves of grace that will impact our family, friends, communities, and world.

When we understand this, and the truth of our calling settles deep within us, we begin to ask a different set of questions:

How does my new identity in Christ shape the purpose of my life?

Who are the people I can impact with the grace of God?

What part will I play in the kingdom of God?

THE PROCESS OF BEING UNVEILED

In the 2010 movie in which Russell Crowe plays the mythical character Robin Hood, I find a striking illustration of all this. Robin, who is adopted by a family in Nottingham in northern England, courageously brings justice to a land under the sway of a foolish and twisted king. Orphaned at an early age, Robin had no idea where he had been born and no idea of his true heritage. At a critical point in the story, however, Marion's father helps Robin discover his identity. He learns that he was the son of a revolutionary father who had lived to bring a better life to his people, only to be killed by evil and powerful men. His father had coined the phrase, "Until Lambs Become Lions," a slogan that revealed that his father had the heart of a shepherd and a longing for justice.

Through that experience, Robin learned his family name and reconnected with his people. In so doing, he not only found out who he was, but something deep within him was ignited with a purpose that had been destined for him from an early age. This newly recognized destiny gave him the courage to live with freedom and passion. He came to believe that his life could count for something.

Can't each of us identify with Robin Hood's longing for an understanding of identity and life's destiny? John Eldredge acknowledges this same quest. Eldredge wrote, "We are in the process of being unveiled. We were created to reflect God's glory, born to bear his image, and he ransomed us to reflect that glory again. Every heart was given a mythic glory, and that glory is being restored."[5]

Near the end of Jesus' life, He was able to say in prayer to His heavenly Father, "I have brought you glory on earth by completing the work you gave me to do" (John 17:4). At the end of our lives, will we be able to say something similar, with confidence? Of King David it was said, "For when David had served God's purpose in his own generation, he fell asleep" (Acts 13:36). I believe the Scriptures promise us the same opportunity. When we leave this earthly home at the end of our days, we can have confidence that we have served God's purposes for us.

I pray for the days to return when the onlooking world would marvel at the power of God resident in and through His people! God's people, including YOU, were designed to *make waves* in your world — waves of grace.

In the pages that follow, you will learn where your kingdom influence and contribution lie. My longing for this book is that God will use it as an instrument of freedom, releasing you to discover your divinely directed destiny. No matter where you are in your spiritual journey, the words on these pages are meant to paint a clear picture of what a grace-filled life is meant to be like and to help you see the powerful contribution God has prepared you to make in His world.

Are you ready to make some waves?

PART 1

CRASHING WAVES

Where We Are Broken for His Good Purposes

CHAPTER 1

BROKENNESS OPENS THE DOOR

When we accept ownership of our powerlessness and helplessness, when we acknowledge that we are paupers at the door of God's mercy, then God can make something beautiful out of us.
— BRENNAN MANNING

DURING A VACATION a few years ago, Pam and I had the opportunity to bask in the sun and surf along the beautiful coast near La Jolla, California. When friends invited us to go sea kayaking, we jumped at the chance for a new adventure. As the two of us shared a sea kayak we watched a school of dolphins go by. A little later, some seals and sea lions entertained us, barking one-liners from an outcropping of rock.

The afternoon proceeded swimmingly until we hit some rough waters on our way back to the beach. We were paddling in with great determination and didn't notice the five-foot wave curling toward us. Our friend Jill shouted a cry of warning just in time for us to look up into the sea-green underbelly of a watery monster cascading down upon us. Our kayak rolled. We tumbled head over heels and took a face-first tour of the ocean floor. Once we determined which way was up, we swam frantically to recover our paddles and kayaks. Finally we both made our way sputtering and spewing to the beach and began to wipe the sand from our eyes and ears and noses.

It doesn't take many years on the planet for us to realize that God does not always hold back the crashing waves that slam into our lives. But the Scripture tells us that God can use rogue waves for His good purposes. In fact, in God's kingdom, we are only prepared to be used by Him through "death" experiences; times when we are brought to the end of ourselves. Jesus said, "I tell you the truth, unless a kernel of wheat falls to the ground and dies, it remains only a single seed. But if it dies, it produces many seeds" (John 12:24). He tells us we can't make waves of grace until we have come to the point of experiencing God's grace through brokenness and dependence.

HAPPY DEAD-ENDINGS

Those dead ends in our lives are often just the places God wants to meet us. Shortly after we graduated from college, my wife, Pam, and I moved to Denver, where we began helping out at a church that was just being birthed. It was an exciting, time of hearing God's voice, living by faith, and getting a chance to lend our gifts in a fresh and vital ministry setting. But similar to the day sea kayaking, we were oblivious to the tsunami ahead.

After a while, this new church hired us to direct their student ministry efforts among junior high, high school, and college students. We saw many young people coming to faith and enjoyed several challenging and invigorating years loving and serving students and families. We saw students begin to follow Jesus and many of them grew deeply grounded as His followers. On Sunday mornings during those years I led a small college-aged class on the topic of sharing faith in Christ. One Sunday, we made plans to meet at a local restaurant for the lesson.

I'm not sure if it was the change of venue, the cloudy weather that morning, or the topic of discussion, but just one person showed up: Martha. Martha had never been to the group before; she had just seen the announcement for that morning's gathering in the church bulletin and decided to come. Pam and I welcomed her and began a friendly conversation. We soon learned that Martha had lived a very difficult life. Her parents were divorced. She was estranged from them, and she was struggling to earn enough income to live and to pay for the classes she was taking at a nearby community college. Life had not been kind to Martha; and she was broken, desperate, and in need of rescue.

We ordered breakfast, and as we waited I tried to figure out how I would conduct the class with only one in attendance. Very quickly, it became obvious that Martha was not yet acquainted with Jesus Christ. She was an overwhelmed young woman desperately looking for help. Her decision to come to the class was a rather random attempt to grab at anything that might give her answers in a life that was out of control. During breakfast I talked with Martha about her life and tried to help her understand God's love for her. We talked about God's interest in her and His ability to enter into her current crisis. That morning at the restaurant, Martha understood and responded to God's love for her in Christ. She made a decision to follow Jesus, and in the weeks and months to come joined other young women in a Bible study, where she began to grow as a follower of Christ.

These days in Denver were enormously satisfying and encouraging. Opportunities to see God move and bring others to faith occurred again and again, and Pam and I were awed and humbled to be involved. After several years, however, we learned that some influential people in the church, including some elders and senior staff members, were dissatisfied with our leadership. After participating in a six-month review conducted by the church staff, we were asked to resign, along with other staff we had hired. The experience was extremely difficult and discouraging.

I was depressed, felt unappreciated and misunderstood, and ultimately felt like a failure. The decision to fire us, along with the reasons

supporting the decision, was announced by the church leadership in
front of the three thousand people we had served. We were absolutely
shattered as the wave crashed over us. But through it all I came to
realize that the very brokenness that brought Martha to the end of
herself and ultimately to Christ was leading me to know Him deeper.
Once the fog cleared I saw more clearly the imperfections I had
brought to the job and the missteps I had made during the process.
Even so, it took quite some time to get over the pain and the feelings
of betrayal and anger. Ultimately God provided opportunities to rec-
oncile and come to greater understanding of the decisions made.

Despite plenty of weaknesses and blind spots, up to that point in
life I had not experienced failures like this one. I had done well in
school, had trophies to show for various athletic pursuits, and had
married a beautiful and relationally gifted woman. Yet God knew
what I needed. He knew the pride and self-dependence that lurked
not far beneath the surface. I now realize that God used those events
to break me and form me in Christ. Given a choice between skipping
that heart-rending season or any successes since, I would choose to
keep those months of pain. I see the resultant growth and ongoing
blessing of having been broken, shown my weakness, and humbled.

As A. W. Tozer has said, "It is doubtful that God will use a person
greatly whom He has not hurt deeply." I don't know if God will ever
use me in great ways, but I do know that any worthwhile fruit borne
through my life is due in part to those dark days. The Bible is filled
with such happy dead-endings. In the gospel of Mark, Jesus came
upon a man suffering with leprosy. The man kneeled before Jesus and
begged him for help, saying, "If you are willing, you can make me
clean" (Mark 1:40). Three things stand out about this man as he
approached Jesus.

- *He recognized his weakness.* This man was a leper, but not a
  stupid leper! Physicians of the day did not call the
  neighborhood Walgreens with a prescription for treating

leprosy. This suffering man knew that without a miracle he would not get well.

- *He pursued Christ.* He did not wallow in his doubt or discouragement. He found a way to drag his sore and ravaged self to Jesus. Likewise, when we see our need, we need to take that need to Christ.
- *He acted out of humility.* He "begged him on his knees" (Mark 1:40). Coming to Christ with our needs is a humbling experience, and at times it can even feel humiliating. Our culture rewards self-sufficiency, not vulnerability and humility. Coming to God for help may even mean losing face in front of other people. This man with leprosy knew well his need for healing and rescue. He took steps to go to Jesus. He presented himself humbly before Him.

Jesus, upon seeing this humble man who recognized his need, was filled with compassion. The leprous man was healed that day.

I could tell story after story of modern-day broken people I've had the privilege to know who came to a place of need and made a decision to put their trust in Christ. Some are first-timers in the faith, folks who've never trusted Christ before. Others are long-time believers who finally come to the end of their rope of self sufficiency because of a work crisis, marriage challenge, or a parenting dilemma. In each situation it is brokenness, weakness, and trials that lead to humility and set the stage for a deeper experience of God's care and grace. Likewise those who make waves of grace most readily are those who have gained credibility through their own suffering.

ENTERING THE KINGDOM EMPTY

Nowhere in the Bible is this principle more plain than in the beatitudes. Martyn Lloyd-Jones, in his commentary on the Sermon on the Mount, contends that the beatitudes are not a random list of characteristics portraying followers of Jesus. Instead, each beatitude builds upon the last. He writes this of the first beatitude, "Blessed are the poor in spirit" (Matthew 5:3):

> *There is no one in the kingdom of God who is* not *poor in spirit. It is the fundamental characteristic of the Christian and of the citizen of the kingdom of heaven, and all the other characteristics are in a sense the result of this one. . . . We shall see that it really means an emptying, while the others are a manifestation of a fullness. We cannot be filled until we are first empty.*[1]

Remember the leper and his response to a life-depleting burden? When have you last begged Jesus on your knees for the deliverance and rescue that He alone can bring? Experiencing the kingdom of God begins when we admit our desperate need for a savior. When we admit that our immorality and brokenness in thought, deed, emotion, and intent leaves us needy and lost apart from Him. Christian spirituality apart from brokenness and admitting our poverty is empty religion and just another form of life built on human effort, and often the pride of self-accomplishment.

The difference between Christ and all other forms of religion is grace; the truth that life is found when we admit we are empty apart from the life, power, and redemptive work of Jesus Christ. Calvin Miller describes this dynamic: "Pride sucks the vitality out of our character. Bernard of Clairvaux wisely taught that there are four Christian virtues. The first is humility. The second is humility. The third is humility. And the fourth is humility. Bernard also taught that most of us would like to gain humility without humiliation. Alas, it is not possible."[2]

But we don't have to stay shattered in our brokenness or wallow in our weakness. For those who come to Him in weakness, God has plans to make us into something new, people who reflect Him and His goodness. It is this kind of person God uses in a hope-needy world. We are not relegated to desperation, but instead we are exalted as a people who have hope because we are connected to the One who brings light out of darkness, fruitfulness out of barrenness, and beauty out of ashes.

QUESTIONS FOR REFLECTION

- What "dead-endings" or significant difficulties has God used to bring you to a place of greater dependence on Him?
- When you are going through difficulties or challenges in life, what keeps you from recognizing your weakness and coming more quickly to humbly ask Jesus for help?

CHAPTER 2

BEAUTY INSTEAD OF ASHES

This happened that we might not rely on ourselves but on God, who raises the dead.

— PAUL (2 CORINTHIANS 1:9)

I MOVED AROUND a lot as a child and teenager. In those days the big company my father worked for intentionally developed their leaders through exposure to new environments and greater challenges. This translated into multiple "transfers" to new divisions and new cities for our family. We moved nine times in eighteen years, I lived in nine different homes before I went to college. As a result of all these moves I can shoot a hockey puck, speak with a Texas drawl, and tell you right where the Rock and Roll Hall of Fame is. But, as you might imagine, these relocations were often very difficult. On a number of occasions I suffered from severe loneliness.

Mark Twain once suggested that upon becoming a teenager a kid should be stuck in a wood barrel with a hole drilled in the side for air. He then went on to suggest that at age sixteen the hole should be sealed with a cork. Apparently Twain didn't have a very high estimation of teenagers. My own story might convince others of Twain's wisdom. I was about to enter my freshman year of high school. At the end of the summer, a group of teenage guys (my "friends") began systematically and publically depantsing different guys in our little group. A couple of the ringleaders were exempt, but everyone else had to be on their toes. Each weekend a new guy would be their target. I hadn't participated but had heard about their antics and lived in fear that I might be next.

As it turned out, my fears were well founded. One weekend we were spending time goofing around. Late at night, when we started getting bored, one of the guys suggested they get me. I tried to outrun them but finally got caught. They stole my clothes from the waist down—but gave them back after they got their laugh. It was a traumatic experience. I was made fun of and ridiculed, even a week later by students on the bus. It was a soul-crushing experience.

I would have been delighted for our family to receive a transfer immediately after that experience, but most of the time I dreaded the moves. As I grew older, it became even harder to make new friends. I lacked confidence and found it more and more difficult to resist peer pressure. We moved between my sophomore and junior year of high school to a suburb of Cleveland, Ohio. It was the most difficult move yet. I was not yet a follower of Christ, and during those final years of high school I struggled and gave into various sexual temptations and experimented with alcohol and drugs. I was vulnerable and broken, hungry for love and help, not knowing that God had plans for a better future.

A PORTRAIT OF THE HEART OF GOD

If my story is moving to you, it's probably because some aspects of it remind you of your own. Hard circumstances yield hard lessons and painful memories. Isaiah 61 is a passage Jesus used to reach people like us in our brokenness. At the inauguration of His ministry in a synagogue in Nazareth, Jesus used this Old Testament text to paint a vivid portrait of the good news of God and God's heart for those who need Him. As you read this text, note the theme of redemption and restoration, God bringing newness and healing and freedom out of crushing circumstances:

> *The Spirit of the Sovereign LORD is on me,*
> *because the LORD has anointed me*
> *to preach good news to the poor.*
> *He has sent me to bind up the brokenhearted,*
> *to proclaim freedom for the captives*
> *and release from darkness for the prisoners,*
> *to proclaim the year of the LORD's favor*
> *and the day of vengeance of our God,*
> *to comfort all who mourn,*
> *and provide for those who grieve in Zion —*
> *to bestow on them a crown of beauty*
> *instead of ashes,*
> *the oil of gladness*
> *instead of mourning,*
> *and a garment of praise*
> *instead of a spirit of despair.*
> *They will be called oaks of righteousness,*
> *a planting of the LORD*
> *for the display of his splendor.* (Isaiah 61:1-3)

In this passage, we find three wonderful descriptions of people to whom God offers His help:

First, the good news is for the brokenhearted. In every part of the world it is hard to go far without seeing brokenhearted people. And if we are honest, we'll admit that we too have experienced our own heartaches and losses. Family, career, health, and relationships are the crucibles we all have in common, in which our hearts are crushed.

Second, we see that the good news of God is available for people who are in captivity. There are many kinds of captivity in this world. Certainly many are literally incarcerated. But for others, the imprisonment exists in our spirit. Many of us are captive to anxiety, unforgiveness, depression, or substance or sexual addictions. God's good news is meant to set us free.

Third, we know that many people are shackled in a dungeon of darkness. They have not experienced the light of God found in Jesus Christ. For people without Christ, the god of this age, the devil, longs to keep people blind and in the dark. In describing the gospel, Paul writes, "For he has rescued us from the dominion of darkness and brought us into the kingdom of the Son he loves" (Colossians 1:13). Those without Christ are prisoners in darkness. However, in John 8:12, Jesus describes Himself as "the world's Light. No one who follows me stumbles around in the darkness. I provide plenty of light to live in" (MSG).

Consider Christ's promise to us, that He will bestow, "a crown of beauty instead of ashes." What an outstanding picture of what the good news of Jesus and the kingdom is meant to produce in the lives of Christ followers. When we come to Jesus as poor, brokenhearted captives, prisoners of darkness, He greets us with good news, healing, freedom, release, and comfort. He makes us beautiful, and in thankfulness for His mercy we reach out to others with God's grace.

HIS MEDALS OF GRACE

Wilma Rudolph was born prematurely weighing four pounds, into a family already bursting with nineteen brothers and sisters. As a young child she caught infantile paralysis (caused by the polio virus). She recovered, but wore a brace on her left leg and foot that had become twisted as a result of the disease. By the time she was twelve, she had also survived scarlet fever, whooping cough, chicken pox, and measles. In such a large family, the resources were simply not available for heroic medical measures.

At age twelve, despite the odds against her, Wilma began to shed her braces and use her withered legs. She went from walking to running. In fact, under the guidance of an encouraging doctor and a track coach, she became a very good runner. During the 1960 Olympic games Wilma Rudolph won three gold medals and was labeled the fastest woman in the world, paving the way for women's track in the United States.

Through the gospel, God desires to do the same thing for us. He wants to take us from circumstances of brokenness to the heights of knowing Him through the healing and transformation that He alone performs. He wants to make of our twisted lives His own medals of grace.

I love these words from the song "Losin' Is Winnin'" by John Fischer. They express so well the redemptive work of God in the lives of ordinary people,

> Losin' is winnin' if it turns you around
> It all looks clearer when you're close to the ground
> If you know you're lost then you can be found
> And you walk out a winner.[1]

In the remarkable economy of God, the losers win. The Scriptures brim with story after story of men and women who apart from God's help were without hope. Consider this list of losers: Abraham, Moses, Esther, David, Nehemiah, the woman at the well, the apostle Paul (formerly known as Saul). Each was rescued by God and went on to make waves of grace for God's kingdom that reached far beyond the lands in which they once hung their heads in shame.

THE HENCHMAN TURNED APOSTLE

I cannot finish this chapter without mentioning Saul of Tarsus. He was not the kind of man you would invite over for dinner and a movie. He was a religious zealot who was bound and determined to see the fledgling Jesus movement squashed. He was the Pharisees' premier henchman. When the first early-church martyr recorded in the Scriptures was brutally stoned to death while reciting Old Testament Bible accounts, "Saul was there, giving approval to his death" (Acts 8:1). Acts 9:1-2 paints an even clearer picture:

Meanwhile, Saul was still breathing out murderous threats against the Lord's disciples. He went to the high priest and asked him for letters to the synagogues in Damascus, so that if he found any there who belonged to the Way, whether men or women, he might take them as prisoners to Jerusalem.

And then things changed. Saul experienced a revolutionary change of life! The book of Acts tells of Saul's encounter with Jesus on the road to Damascus, his miraculous conversion, and his calling to become a messenger of Christ. Saul's life made a sharp turnaround, a true life portrayal of Isaiah 61. Captive to a murderous way of life, upon meeting Jesus Christ he was broken and found a new purpose in a life of grace and freedom.

Saul (who adopted the Greek name Paul) later wrote to the new believers in Ephesus, "God saved you by his grace when you believed. And you can't take credit for this; it is a gift from God" (Ephesians 2:8, NLTSE). Paul understood that salvation is not a reward for the good things we have done, so none of us can boast. Instead, "We are God's masterpiece. He has created us anew in Christ Jesus, so we can do the good things he planned for us long ago" (Ephesians 2:9-10, NLTSE). The apostle Paul had a firm grip on the fact that his life was an example of beauty out of ashes, a masterpiece drawn out of the ash heap of a murderer.

With Paul's transformation came great confidence in God and a willingness to live out his faith with abandon! He took the good news all around the Roman world. Along the way, in order to keep him grounded in Christ, God provided him with ample opportunities to find himself desperate. In 2 Corinthians he reflects on the hardships he faced in Asia:

We do not want you to be uninformed, brothers, about the hardships we suffered in the province of Asia. We were under great pressure, far beyond our ability to endure, so that we despaired even of life. Indeed, in our hearts we felt the sentence of death. But this happened that we might not rely on ourselves but on God, who raises the dead. He has delivered us from such a deadly peril, and he will deliver us. On him we have set our hope that he will continue to deliver us, as you help us by your prayers. (1:8-11)

Paul wisely recognized that the hardships, pressures, and desperate situations he faced were good tools, used by God to build his faith. The fires of his confidence in God's deliverance were stoked each time God acted to bring good out of trial, hope out of despair, and beauty out of ashes.

By his example and by his teaching, the waves of grace God began through Paul continue to our day. For those who claim faith, God promises a similarly grand makeover. Like Paul, your influence and destiny as a follower of Christ flows out of ash-stained weakness. May you be filled with great expectancy and trust in God's ability to make something new and beautiful of your life.

QUESTIONS FOR REFLECTION

- As you look back over your life, name personal shortcomings, weaknesses, or areas of sin that you have needed God to help you overcome.
- Pray for God's help in turning these areas of life into a crown of beauty instead of ashes.

CHAPTER 3

THE LITTLE ONES
GOD USES

The least of you will become a thousand, the smallest a mighty nation. I am the LORD; in its time I will do this swiftly.

— ISAIAH 60:22

GOD FREQUENTLY DEMONSTRATES His power by using small instruments to accomplish big purposes.

Early on in the Tolkien trilogy, THE LORD OF THE RINGS, Middle Earth is in desperate straits. The evil Lord Sauron has possession of two magic rings. If the third ring falls into his hands, Middle Earth will not withstand his fury. The elfin leader Elrond oversees a council of men, dwarves, elves, and hobbits including Gandalf, the wizard, to discuss who will take the magic ring and cast it back into the fires of Mordor. The discussion soon grows heated. Personal ambitions and concerns about the futility of the task are forcefully voiced. As the various kingdom representatives stand their ground and raise their voices, a noisy squabble erupts.

Then, suddenly, a small voice demands the attention of all parties: "I'll take the ring to Mordor," says the diminutive Frodo Baggins, a hobbit from the area known as the Shire, "though I do not know the way." What a picture of courage and humility! This three-foot hobbit answered the call to save Middle Earth. Soon Frodo had a group of companions volunteering to accompany him on his mission, henceforth known as the Fellowship of the Ring. This band included many more substantial and seemingly gifted trekkers than Frodo. Aragorn and Boromir represented humankind; there was also Gimli, the dwarf; Legolas, the elf; Gandalf; and three other hobbit friends.

It's Frodo I relate to in that story, though I haven't frequently silenced arguments by volunteering to march into danger. In the last chapter, I shared one of my high school experiences and told about the challenges I faced moving from city to city growing up. By my sophomore year in high school I had been through some tough transitions. As a freshman in a Texas high school outside of Houston, I was four foot eleven and weighed about a hundred pounds. Nevertheless, I went out for football, which either shows my courage or lack of any real intelligence! Texas is the promised land of high school football, and I'm convinced that some of the guys on my team had been shaving since kindergarten. I was able to make a lasting impression on the team however. During one of the first practices I was knocked out cold—during a tackling drill!

That same year, like many young guys, I struggled with how to interact with the opposite sex. I still wince to remember the words of a close friend's girlfriend. She was trying her best to encourage me in my attempts to find a date for homecoming. "Doug," she said, "you know, you are kind of cute. Some day, when you grow up, girls might actually like you." *Ouch!* Suffice it to say, I lacked confidence, and more importantly, I was not yet convinced that God could use a guy like me for much of anything.

MUTTS AND RUNTS, GOD'S VIPS

Every one of us has dealt with feelings of inadequacy and the fear and anxiety associated with them. But the truth we find in Scripture is that just as God must sometimes break us down to make us useful, He never wants us to place our confidence solely in ourselves. This too is by His design.

The book of Judges is packed with stories of lackluster leaders who were not at all the heroic celebrities who would land today's leading movie roles. In fact, if any did get a final audition, they would first need an extreme makeover! Israel simply did not have a king or leader capable of holding the nation together, thus surrounding nations like the Ammonites and Midianites posed a constant threat.

Gideon came on the scene only after Israel's lack of capable leaders and disobedience caused God to hand the entire nation over to the Midianites (see Judges 6:1). Things had gotten so bad that out of fear the Israelites were living in caves. And whenever they planted their crops, the Midianites would attack and ruin them. One bleak day, Gideon was hiding in his family's winepress, processing not grapes but wheat. The only explanation for this strange behavior was that Gideon was trying to keep the Midianites from stealing the threshed grain! Just in the nick of time for Gideon and his kin, an angel of the Lord appeared. The angel called Gideon to be God's instrument to save Israel from the Midianites.

Gideon's response to the angel's invitation indicates that Gideon was still severely lacking in star power. "But Lord," he whined, "how can I save Israel? My clan is the weakest in Manasseh, and I am the least in my family" (Judges 6:15). Gideon's tribe came from one of the two half-tribes that were the offspring of Joseph (from the book of Genesis) and an Egyptian. That lineage was not exactly the kind of pedigree we might expect for God's chosen instrument. Not many Israelites would have argued with Gideon when he admitted that he didn't feel up to the job of hero. Certainly offspring from the other tribes of Israel seemed better suited than he!

But that day God had His eye on the underdog. Three lessons come to my mind in this account of God making Gideon His man of the hour.

First, God sees us through His eyes, not ours. The angel of the Lord addressed Gideon as a "mighty warrior" (Judges 6:12). God views our true nature and the possibilities that exist. Our vision of ourselves often falls short of His eternal knowledge of what He will accomplish through us.

Second, when God calls, He is not dissuaded by excuses or questions regarding His wisdom or selection. In Judges 6:14, God basically silences Gideon's doubts and says, "Go and save Israel and remember that I am the one sending you!"

Third, God promises Gideon His presence in the battle. God's use of underdogs is perfectly wise because He remains with His unlikely heroes all through the battle.

The story of Gideon shows God's desire and ability to use people who are underrated, undersized, and inexperienced. We could take time and see how God did this again and again, using men and women who were not the ones others would have chosen: Moses, Deborah, Josiah, David, Abigail, Peter, and the list goes on.

MY UNLIKELY VICTORY

My sophomore year of high school I decided to go out for student council, running for the lofty office of parliamentarian. Remember, I had only been in the school district two years, having moved from out of state. To make matters worse, I had moved from the Chicago area, so to all those Texans I was definitely a "yankee." Doubling the odds against me was the fact that a boy named Sammy Campbell was the guy I was running against. He was a longtime resident of the area and was well known. He ran track and played football.

I talked with Spring High School officials and learned the proper procedures for running for student council. I began to assemble a campaign. I thought my posters, which I plastered all over the school, would certainly make me a shoo-in. Each included my great campaign slogan, "Don't be a monkey, vote for Nuenke," along with a picture of a grinning monkey, hand-drawn by my mom.

A good bit of effort and time went into the plan for my speech, which was a big part of the campaign. All candidates gave a speech to the entire student body! I was one of two people running for parliamentarian. Certainly I saw the competition clearly: Sammy was a local sports star, and I was four foot eleven inches and weighed one hundred pounds. I knew I needed an edge, so in my speech I used humor and brought focus to my platform's centerpiece: the need for a smoking lounge.

It was the seventies, after all, and students could smoke in the bathrooms back then. I was not a smoker, but I hated going to the bathroom when it was filled with smoke. As I brought my speech to a crescendo, grandly outlining my plans to meet the needs of both smokers and nonsmokers, I got a standing ovation. Miracle of miracles, people voted for me. Doug Nuenke, clearly not a monkey, won in a landslide.

Now, I can make no claim that God was strategically pulling levers in voting booths at Spring High School, but I do believe that God, even before I was following Him, used that event to teach me. When God wills success for an underdog, even a scrawny late-blooming underdog named Doug, that underdog, if He has any brains at all, learns a lesson. He learns about himself and he learns about God. There's nothing too difficult for God.

HIS POWER IN OUR WEAKNESS

We need only reflect on the story of David and Goliath to see that the value of "bigger is better" has been around since the beginning of time. No one thought the small-fry shepherd boy stood a chance against the hulking Philistine warrior, Goliath. Of course, they were all wrong, but should such a contest occur today the odds would undoubtedly still be on the big guy.

Western civilization has continued to buy into the idea that the big, smart, beautiful, and talented are the only ones that can make a difference. Political campaigns, the onslaught of advertising, and Hollywood have fanned the flame of this illusion, but God's ways remain as unchanged as He is. The consistent message of Scripture is that God uses the small, the humble, the weak, and the unlikely to fulfill His purposes. We see this nowhere with more clarity than in the writings of the apostle Paul, explaining God's counterintuitive kingdom to the church at Corinth:

> *God chose things the world considers foolish in order to shame those who think they are wise. And he chose things that are powerless to shame those who are powerful. God chose things despised by the world, things counted as nothing at all, and used them to bring to nothing what the world considers important. As a result, no one can ever boast in the presence of God.*
> (1 Corinthians 1:27-29, NLTSE)

Astonishing and surprising words! *Is this what Christianity is about,* they must have thought, *being powerless, despised nothings?* Later, in his final thoughts to them at the end of 2 Corinthians, he gives personal testimony to the same truth, speaking of a "thorn in my flesh" (NIV), a limitation that God has given him,

> *Because of the extravagance of those revelations, and so I wouldn't get a big head, I was given the gift of a handicap to keep me in constant touch with my limitations. Satan's angel did his best to get me down; what he in fact did was push me to my knees. No danger then of walking around high and mighty! At first I didn't think of it as a gift, and begged God to remove it. Three times I did that, and then he told me,*
>
> > *My grace is enough; it's all you need.*
> > *My strength comes into its own in your weakness.*

Once I heard that, I was glad to let it happen. I quit focusing on the handicap and began appreciating the gift. It was a case of Christ's strength moving in on my weakness. Now I take limitations in stride, and with good cheer, these limitations that cut me down to size — abuse, accidents, opposition, bad breaks. I just let Christ take over! And so the weaker I get, the stronger I become. (12:7-10, MSG)

ARMANDO'S STORY

In his book *From Brokenness to Community*, Jean Vanier paints another picture of the person God is able to use. Vanier provides the account of a rather atypical gathering of bishops who came to visit a community of young people with profound disabilities. One of the residents was eight-year-old Armando. Abandoned at an early age, the attendants explained that at one point in this young boy's life he would not eat because of his deep loneliness. Vanier recounts his story:

Armando cannot walk or talk and is very small for his age. . . . [When he first came to us] he was desperately thin and was dying from lack of food. After a while in our community where he found people who held him, loved him, and wanted him to live, he gradually began to eat again and to develop in a remarkable way.

He still cannot walk or talk or eat by himself, his body is twisted and broken, and he has a severe mental disability, but when you pick him up, his eyes and his whole body quiver with joy and excitement and say, "I love you." He has a deep therapeutic influence on people.

[At the gathering of bishops] I asked one of [them] if he wanted to hold Armando in his arms. He did. I watched the two of them together as Armando settled into his arms and started to quiver and smile, his little eyes shining. A half hour later I came to see if the bishop wanted me to take back

Armando. "No, no," he replied. I could see that Armando in all his littleness, but with all the power of love in his heart, was touching and changing the heart of that bishop.

Bishops are busy men. They have power and they frequently suffer acts of aggression, so they have to create solid defense mechanisms. But someone like Armando can penetrate the barriers they—and all of us—create around our hearts. Armando can awaken us to love and call forth the well of living water and of tenderness hidden inside of us.

Armando is not threatening . . . he just says, "I love you. I love being with you."[1]

God's ways are not our ways (see Isaiah 55:8). In Isaiah 66 God tells of His mighty ability to create, even pointing to heaven as His throne and to earth, His footstool. Based on that revelation of His power, He asks His followers, "What could you possibly build for me that would top that!?" God then goes on to reveal what He really wants. Sit on the edge of your seat and listen to what it is: "But there *is* something I'm looking for: a person simple and plain, reverently responsive to what I say" (verse 2, MSG).

God delights in using the simple and plain, the weak, the runts, the unlikely ones to send out waves of grace into a world obsessed with outward appearances. If we will raise our hands, trust Him and join Him, He will use us despite the voices in our lives that tell us the opposite.

QUESTIONS FOR REFLECTION

- Read 1 Corinthians 1:27-29. Are there areas of your life—intellectually, physically, socially, or emotionally that you tend to feel "less than" other people? What are they? Pray for God to use these areas to help you grow in your relationship with Him.
- Read 2 Corinthians 12:7-10. God says that His power is made perfect in our weakness. Think of any ways that you have seen God show His strength through your weakness or "smallness."

CHAPTER 4

WHERE GOSPEL SEED SPROUTS

The poor man and woman of the gospel have made peace with their flawed existence. They are aware of their lack of wholeness, their brokenness, the simple fact that they don't have it all together. While they do not excuse their sin, they are humbly aware that sin is precisely what has caused them to throw themselves at the mercy of the Father. They do not pretend to be anything but what they are: sinners saved by grace.

— BRENNAN MANNING

DURING THE YEARS that Pam and I led the youth ministry at a large church in Denver, we took kids and volunteers into various settings to expose them to the social challenges that face our world. We worked with city pastors and other organizations in financially depressed areas of the city. While there were challenges and spiritual needs in our own neighborhoods, we found that students' hearts were more open in settings outside their own. These activities broadened our horizons and provided opportunities for us, as people of faith, to bring hope and love to others whose circumstances were different from our own.

We were also able to take trips to Haiti with high school and college students. Together we learned more about how people live who do not have the financial resources we enjoy. We learned quite a lot about the differences between our western culture of abundance and the Haitians' culture of scarcity. On each trip, we went to serve but came away blessed by people who were rich in culture and spirit.

Sometime after one of those trips, we decided it would be a good idea to organize a reunion activity. We invited the team we had taken to Haiti to a homeless shelter to serve lunch. We got to the shelter ahead of time so that we could help with the meal preparation. About a half hour before lunch a line began to form outside the building and we were able to greet those we were about to serve. Most of the men and women who came were grateful for a warm meal. There were a few exceptions, however.

As we served warm beans and bread, chicken noodle soup, along with a hearty chicken casserole, we couldn't help but compare this to the meals we had served in Haiti: mostly rice gruel and chicken broth. In comparison, this meal was surely a five-star delight, but not every person who passed through our line was delighted with our offerings. "Not that crap again," some said. Others left the food line with hardly a morsel on their plate. Clearly, for some, the food that day was less than inspiring. Perhaps all of us can think of times we've been similarly ungrateful, times when we rejected something perfectly good and walked away empty because our hearts were not rightly oriented.

Numerous times through the years, the following story has played out. On one particular occasion I had an infrequent mentoring opportunity with a recent graduate named Steve (not his real name). He had grown up in Kansas City, so he would return there periodically from his new home in Georgia. On a number of occasions he gave me a call so we could schedule time together. Each time we discussed the challenges he faced in his life and his relationship with the Lord. And each time we met, the news went from bad to worse. From the day Steve graduated and moved away from many of his spiritual role models in Kansas City, he had struggled with partying and unhealthy relationships with women.

Each time we got together, we talked about the salvation found in Jesus and the power that is available for His children. Steve heard of God's love and willingness to forgive. He heard the promises from Scripture that God would and could set him free from his struggles with temptation and sin. But each time we parted, I could tell that the good words had fallen on bad soil. Steve's longing to fill his life with women and alcohol was much greater than his desire to be delivered. Like the would-be diners at the soup kitchen, Steve's heart was not ready to receive the good things offered him.

A KINGDOM FOR CHILDREN

Jesus knew, of course, that some to whom He spoke would not receive Him, His words, or His work as they ought. In Matthew 19:13-30, Jesus reveals the kind of people who receive the good news of the gospel and those who don't. To begin He exalts some small and unlikely heroes — little children — as His model of faith.

> One day some parents brought their children to Jesus so he could lay his hands on them and pray for them. But the disciples scolded the parents for bothering him.
> But Jesus said, "Let the children come to me. Don't stop them! For the Kingdom of Heaven belongs to those who are like these children." And he placed his hands on their heads and blessed them before he left. (verses 13-15, NLTSE)

In the chapter immediately preceding this one, Matthew included other words of Jesus regarding the merits of childlike faith:

> At that time the disciples came to Jesus and asked, "Who is the greatest in the kingdom of heaven?"
> He called a little child and had him stand among them. And he said: "I tell you the truth, unless you change and

become like little children, you will never enter the kingdom of heaven. Therefore, whoever humbles himself like this child is the greatest in the kingdom of heaven." (Matthew 18:1-4)

What observations can be made about little children and why Jesus would raise them up as examples of faith? Three things come to mind:

First, little children come. Before being hurt by the realities of this world, children have a naïve openness that causes them to run unquestioningly to those who exude safety and welcome.

Second, little children are without pretense. They are humble and do not strive for recognition or praise.

Third, little children are quick to receive good news in whatever form it comes. Whether it's a hug, an ice cream cone, a crayon drawing, a shiny penny, a storybook, or a soft stuffed animal, children enthusiastically receive most any gift given in love. Adults are much more careful about the implications of admitting weakness or having a need for help. They worry about losing face, having a reduced personal stock value, or being seen as weak or insufficient.

Matthew makes this very point when he follows his description of the beauty of childlike faith with a story portraying the obstacles adults face in coming to Jesus. In Matthew 19:16-22, he relates the story of a wealthy young man who approaches Jesus as though he really is looking for "good news" in the form of spiritual advice.

"Teacher," the young man begins, "what good thing must I do to get eternal life?"

Jesus answers by listing some of the Ten Commandments, as well as the command to love one's neighbor as one's self.

"Hey, I'm good," the young man responds. "Anything else?"

Jesus ups the ante. "If you want to give it all you've got," Jesus replies, "go sell your possessions; give everything to the poor. All your wealth will then be in heaven. Then come follow me."

That was the last thing the young man expected to hear. And so, crestfallen, he walked away. He was holding on tight to a lot of things, and he couldn't bear to let go. (verse 22, MSG)

What's the difference between a child and a rich young man's ability to receive "good news"? The humble child comes ready to receive. The rich man doesn't really see his need and consequently does not see what Jesus has to offer as good.

How people experience the good news is an interesting study, and connects to our discussion of brokenness and poverty of spirit. The degree to which we are willing to receive the grace of Christ has a direct effect on how God will use us in our world for the sake of the kingdom.

Jesus Christ is good news. Through His words and works He brought good news to a hurting world. That good news found its fullest expression through His death and resurrection. The New Testament word *gospel* means good news, or glad tidings. It is both the message and the reality of that message heard and experienced by those to whom it comes. Isaiah 52:7 is a great Old Testament gospel verse that tells of those who bring good news and the core message of kingdom good news,

> *How beautiful on the mountains*
> *are the feet of those who bring good news,*
> *who proclaim peace,*
> *who bring good tidings,*
> *who proclaim salvation,*
> *who say to Zion,*
> *"Your God reigns!"*

The gospel of God is the announcement of the peace of God, His good news, His salvation, all of which point to the truth of His reign as King.

The good news of the kingdom connects with people's hearts when they recognize their need and receive the news of what the King has to offer. As such, our ability to receive the good news depends primarily on our humility quotient! We will never make waves of grace, if we cannot humbly receive it ourselves.

PORTRAITS OF GOOD NEWS AND BROKENNESS

In the letters of the apostle Paul, we see so many wonderful metaphors used to describe the good news of Jesus and the kingdom of God. Consider these marvelous words that can bring so much hope to people who come to Jesus:

- *Regeneration* or new life is good news to someone whose life is worn out, broken, and burdened by shame.
- *Salvation* or rescue is good news for someone who knows he is a captive or up against an overpowering enemy.
- *Adoption* is good news to those who are orphans or long for parenting they've not known.
- *Reconciliation* is good news for people who know they are estranged from God.
- *Atonement and Justification* are great news for those who see their sin and know they are guilty.

As incredible as each of these aspects of God's grace is, notice that each one of these is received as good news only to the extent that the recipient realizes his poverty and need. As we touched on earlier, Jesus declared that Isaiah 61 summarized His ministry of good news in the first century:

The Spirit of the Lord is on me,
because he has anointed me
to preach good news to the poor.
He has sent me to proclaim freedom for the prisoners

and recovery of sight for the blind,
to release the oppressed,
    to proclaim the year of the Lord's favor. (Luke 4:18-19)

While there is no question that the good news of Jesus Christ involves our relationship with God and the forgiveness of sins, it is also true that the reign of God, which found such full expression in Jesus' coming to earth, brings physical, emotional, and even culture-transforming good news to people and to our world. Consider the way that Jesus brought good news to each of these people, engaging each of them in a way that acknowledged his or her brokenness:

- For blind Bartimaeus, what was the best imaginable news? "I want to see!" He may not have known his spiritual need before he made his request, but he learned a faith lesson and was following Jesus shortly thereafter (see Mark 10:47,51).
- To the foreign woman, a Greek born in Syrian Phoenicia, good news was getting a hearing with Jesus, the healer. She knew her need and desperately desired the good news (see Mark 7:27-28).
- A demon-possessed man who had the whole countryside shaking in fear fell at Jesus' feet. He wanted only to be set free from spiritual oppression. Did that man experience the good news of Jesus and the kingdom? So much so that he wanted to immediately go and become one of Jesus' disciples, and when he found out that wasn't possible he became the local preacher (see Luke 8:38-39).

GOSPEL SEED NEEDS THE SOIL OF BROKENNESS

I once found myself in a counseling situation with a young man named Carl (not his real name) who was struggling with enslavement to pornography and impure relations with women. He had grown up in a godly home, attending Christian preschool, Sunday school, youth group, youth camps, and conferences. He had attended Bible studies, and there was no question that he was a follower of Jesus and had a great desire to see his life reflect the character of the Lord. Even so, he remained broken and enslaved.

I asked him what it means to be "saved." He responded with well-worn evangelical lingo: "Put your faith in the cross and resurrection of Jesus. Ask for forgiveness of sin and ask Jesus to enter your life." Knowing this young man, his commitment was sincere, but he lacked any note of desperation and had yet to experience the power of Jesus' good news.

I shared with him the fact that most of the time, especially in the Old Testament, the idea of being "saved" means just that, experiencing God's rescue. A writer of the Psalms, reflecting on his own trials, his isolation, and the slander from his enemies, wrote,

> But I trust in you, O LORD;
>   I say, "You are my God."
> My times are in your hands;
>   deliver me from my enemies
>   and from those who pursue me.
> Let your face shine on your servant;
>   save me in your unfailing love. (Psalm 31:14-16)

All of us, in order to have true and life-changing faith, have to get to that utterly broken place where we know we are helpless without Him. For Carl, the good news he needed most was the knowledge and experience that our God is king and reigns over the forces of evil that were leading to his enslavement to pornography. I prayed with him that day that God would rescue him and release him from captivity.

GOOD NEWS FOR EVERYONE, EVERY DAY

Now, all of us do not have so dramatic an enslavement, but our needs are no less great and they affect our lives in ways that make us cry out to God. Over the years, I've come to discover that I too have been taken captive in ways that are as real as being imprisoned. I am a first-born son and my parents passed along the values of hard work and excellence. They encouraged me, sometimes too strongly, to aspire toward those high standards. Dad was an only child, and he had experienced some of the same from his dad. I am so grateful for the values my parents built into my life. However, the high standards they enforced combined with other challenges that were part of my childhood gave me a strong desire to perform and to please people, especially those with influence over me.

One time, as a first grader, I got a "sad face" on a coloring assignment. When I brought that assignment home, my dad copied it and had me redo it several times over. Now I'm sure it may not have been as bad as I remember, but it is one memory that built into me a strong desire to perform. The positive side of all this is it created in me a desire for excellence and an ability to give my all to be my best. The downside is that I often struggle with being a slave to performance and people pleasing. In sharing this I don't mean to suggest that we blame our weaknesses and sins on our past, our parents, or people that hurt us. I can't imagine growing to manhood without my parents' guidance and love. However, I've found it helpful to know the sources of my pain and the things that hinder me, as I acknowledge my need for Christ to bring healing and teach me a better way.

Because of my background and the lies I have believed about my identity and value, I tend to find purpose in being right and getting things right. At times I can work more than I should and have too much of an eye for detail—often for the sake of looking good, performing well, and "getting it right."

Good news for me is finding out that peace and wholeness is not found in perfection or being right, but in experiencing the love of God as His adopted son. Colossians 3:3-4, which I quote to myself almost every day, says, "For you died, and your life is now hidden with Christ in God. When Christ, *who is your life*, appears, then you also will appear with him in glory" (emphasis added). I can only be released from my captivity to performance addiction when I admit that I am a prisoner. God rescues me, whispering to me that I am His child, that I am worthwhile, and that I am loved by Him before I ever set a foot out of bed in the morning.

Jesus offers Himself to each of us this way with each new day, if we'll only receive Him with grateful hearts, acknowledging our real need. He is good news and provides good news — rescue, deliverance, healing, hope, forgiveness of sins, and eternal life — to all who embrace it with humble faith. His waves of grace are sufficient for every moment of our lives.

The words of John Fischer's song, "Beggar," express the heart that is good soil for the seed of the good news whenever we need it . . .

I know where the food is
And it isn't very far away
Doesn't cost much but an empty soul
And the pride that stands in the way

I'm not one who's got it all in place
Telling you what you should do
No I'm just one old hungry beggar
Showing you where I found food

Have you found the water
That will never make you thirst again
Jesus is a well of water springing up
Into eternal life from within

I'm not one who's got it all in place
Telling you what you should do
No I'm just one old hungry beggar
Showing you where I found food

Maybe you aren't hungry
And maybe you don't thirst at all
But maybe the years have hardened the tears
And you really are a beggar after all

I'm not one who's got it all in place
Telling you what you should do
No I'm just one old hungry beggar
Showing you where I found food.[1]

In this "Crashing Waves" section, we have seen that brokenness and humility are prerequisites for fully experiencing Christ and the kingdom of God. Brokenness is the doorway to the kingdom. Jesus promises to bring good out of hardship, hope out of despair, and beauty out of ashes. He will set us free as we bring our chains and captivity to Him. God is not limited to using the rich, famous, strong, or beautiful to accomplish His purposes. In fact, He finds delight in using the "little ones." God uses the weak to fulfill His plans. We experience the kingdom of God and move toward our destiny and usefulness when we embrace the good news of Christ and His reign like little children. God's power is best seen and experienced when His people most fully know their desperate need for Him.

QUESTIONS FOR REFLECTION

- Consider the kind of dependence little children have on their parents. What makes it difficult for you to rely on Christ with this kind of dependence?
- Reflect on these words that describe God's work in the gospel: *new birth, rescue, adoption, reconciliation, forgiveness.* Which of these do you particularly need to experience more fully?

PART 2

STREAMS OF FRESH WATER

Where Our Longing for God Is Satisfied

CHAPTER 5

BECAUSE HE FIRST LOVED US

My chains fell off, my heart was free, I rose, went forth, and followed Thee.

— CHARLES WESLEY

BY THE SECOND day of a backpacking trip with two friends in the southern reaches of Grand Teton National Park, we found ourselves up high in the hills on the backside of those majestic peaks and our supply of clean water had almost run out. We began looking for a fresh source. The year had been dry, so many of the streams and creeks that should have provided fresh water were dry or underground. We were going eight to twelve miles a day, mostly uphill, above ten-thousand feet, and carrying forty pounds of provisions. The air was thin and that day we were feeling especially parched. We prayed for God to supply our need.

Around noon, we were hiking close to tree line. We stopped to put on our rain gear, noticing in the heights beyond us a thunderstorm moving quickly in our direction. At first when we stopped, we noticed no sound but the breeze blowing through the pines. But then we heard another distinct sound, the trickle and splash of water. We moved toward the sound, and soon rounded a rock outcropping to find a flow of water cascading down a previously dry creek bed. The high country storm had released enough rain to reinvigorate the creek. We had more than enough water to replenish our bottles.

Throughout Scripture the metaphor of thirst is used to describe the core of our spiritual need, the longings of our hearts. While men and women often try to quench their thirst with other things, the Christ follower learns that there is only one true source of living water able to satiate that longing. Recall the words of Jesus at the great feast in Jerusalem as He revealed who He is and what He provides for those who put their hope in Him: "If anyone is thirsty, let him come to me and drink. Whoever believes in me, as the Scripture has said, streams of living water will flow from within him" (John 7:37-38).

In part 1, we focused on humble and broken dependence as the key characteristics of those who approach Christ. Here in part 2, we will take the next step together. We move from thirst to satisfaction, as we consider what characterizes people who long after God and pursue Him for the waters of life. Just as contrite and tried believers are able to genuinely influence others for Christ, so too only those filled with the living waters of Christ will have something to offer a world thirsty for relationship with God.

On the eve of His crucifixion, during an intimate time with His closest disciples, Jesus reminded them of this very truth. He said, "I am the Vine, you are the branches. When you're joined with me and I with you, the relation intimate and organic, the harvest is sure to be abundant. Separated, you can't produce a thing" (John 15:5, MSG). If we want to be people who are used by God to pass along the waves of His grace, we must be drawing life from Him.

We begin this part of our journey at the core of our life in Christ. What's your motive for seeking a deeper relationship with Christ? Do "shoulds" and "ought tos" drive your faith walk? Are you driven, as I often am, to please others with your performance? Is your spiritual life a task checklist or a pleasure? What drives you to know, worship, and serve God?

It is possible for wrong motives to dam up the flow of God's grace in and through our lives.

OUTRAGEOUS DEVOTION

In Luke 7 we see a drama unfold in which Jesus gives us profound insight into our motivations for loving God. A prostitute enters the home of a religious leader where Jesus is dining. Tension fills the room as values collide! It was bold enough for this woman to even show her face in such "holy" surroundings, but her further actions are even more scandalous! She walks around behind Jesus, kneels, and weeps in repentance at His feet. She wipes his feet with her unbound hair, the long and free-flowing hair that characterized a woman of her profession at that time. She anoints His feet with expensive perfume, worth as much as several month's wages. It is a bold and outrageous display of devotion.

The group of religious men there with Jesus certainly equated right spirituality with right behavior and proper performance. In this situation they were faced with a woman who clearly broke the rules. Her behavior was relational and spontaneous. One of the men, deeply offended, responded, "If this man was the prophet I thought he was, he would have known what kind of woman this is who is falling all over him" (Luke 7:39, MSG). The religious leaders had no idea where to file this woman's display of over-the-top devotion, but we understand that Jesus had deeply influenced this woman's life. She found herself not neck-deep in judgment but miraculously loved by Jesus and given the opportunity to love Him in return. From her display of affection we see three indications of a rescued soul:

First, we can only be rescued when we recognize our need and it shows in our repentant disposition. This woman was not avoiding Jesus, although in shame and embarrassment that might be an understandable response. Instead she courageously entered a place that was way outside her comfort zone, both because of her low social standing and the judgmental nature of the religious leaders. She took that risk because she knew that the One who brought her grace was also there.

Second, a rescued person shows extravagant love for the rescuer. Worship and thanks are the most natural responses to unmerited and unbridled love and rescue.

Third, someone who has been truly rescued doesn't care what others think about their affection for their rescuer.

In the midst of the drama played out between the grateful woman and the questioning Pharisees, Jesus took the opportunity to teach those present a lesson about motivation. He told a parable:

> *"Two men owed money to a certain moneylender. One owed him five hundred denarii, and the other fifty. Neither of them had the money to pay him back, so he canceled the debts of both. Now which of them will love him more?"*
>
> *Simon replied, "I suppose the one who had the bigger debt canceled."*
>
> *"You have judged correctly," Jesus said.* (Luke 7:41-43)

Then Jesus made a masterful segue. Turning toward the woman, he spoke to Simon:

> *Do you see this woman? I came into your house. You did not give me any water for my feet, but she wet my feet with her tears and wiped them with her hair. You did not give me a kiss, but this woman, from the time I entered, has not stopped kissing my feet. You did not put oil on my head, but she has poured perfume on my feet. Therefore, I tell you, her many sins have been forgiven—for she loved much. But he who has been forgiven little loves little.* (Luke 7:44-47)

Likewise, our longing and motivation to pursue God is a response to His love for us. Our own rescue results in a life that honors and reflects the heart of our great Rescuer. Those who operate under the weight of rules have lost touch with what rescue feels like, and they often don't understand the passion and pursuit of those who do. Paul uncovered the same thing among certain law-focused zealots he unmasked among the church at Rome: "Or do you show contempt for the riches of his kindness, tolerance and patience, not realizing that God's kindness leads you toward repentance?" (Romans 2:4). The Pharisees' performance-based system left their souls parched, while this woman found that she was loved by Jesus and loved Him in response. As John put it so succinctly, "We love because he first loved us" (1 John 4:19).

DR PEPPER AND DESIRE FOR GOD

Periodically, when I'm leading a discussion group, I'll ask people to describe a time when they really hit bottom and clung only to God. Some people struggle with answering that question. For some, affluence seems to provide a shield from dire need. Others recognize that it's possible that some of the good things of life, such as material possessions, friends, success, talent, or beauty, can actually become barriers that keep them from fully depending on God and fully experiencing His love.

No doubt, many of us are motivated to honor and seek God by a desire to be obedient and a recognition that He reigns as King of our lives along with all He has made. However, if what Jesus said is true—that those who are forgiven much will love much—might it also be true that those who experience the rescue of God most dramatically will be the most motivated to long after Him? This seems to be reflected in the prophet Jeremiah's words to Judah,

> Long ago the LORD said to Israel:
> "I have loved you, my people, with an everlasting love.
> With unfailing love I have drawn you to myself."
> (Jeremiah 31:3, NLTSE)

It seems that the most sincere motivation for pursuing God and loving Him is the natural response of a loved and rescued child. We love Him and want to be with Him because we are drawn by His love and grace. Throughout Scripture we see these two different motivations for devotion. We see men and women who pursue God by following performance-based religion and we see true, God-loving spirituality that is a response to God's grace and His sacrifice on our behalf.

In Psalm 51:14-17, God reveals His preference through the words of David,

> *Commute my death sentence, God, my salvation God,*
> *and I'll sing anthems to your life-giving ways.*
> *Unbutton my lips, dear God;*
> *I'll let loose with your praise.*
>
> *Going through the motions doesn't please you,*
> *a flawless performance is nothing to you.*
> *I learned God-worship*
> *when my pride was shattered.*
> *Heart-shattered lives ready for love*
> *don't for a moment escape God's notice.* (MSG)

I grew up attending church, but the Christianity I saw as a child caused me to feel guilty and persuaded me that the only proper response was to work hard to make up for my sins. Perhaps I misinterpreted what was taught in my church, but that was how I experienced religion as a young boy. My lips were not unbuttoned as David's were because I truly did not understand the grace of God.

As I touched on earlier, I came to faith in Christ my freshman year of college through the influence and words of friends who were authentic lovers of Jesus. I came into the kingdom when I realized the amazing story of the Cross and love of Christ. I was amazed that God would love people so much that He would die for them. I found myself highly motivated to know Him, learn as much as I could about Him, serve Him, and tell others about His incredible love. Like a young child who first discovers Dr Pepper or chocolate cake, I was juiced up and ready to invite everyone I knew to give it a try. In those earliest days of new life, mine was not a dry religion built on performance and attendance but a life-altering exposure to astounding love.

Over the Thanksgiving holidays during my freshman year, I traveled from TCU in Fort Worth down to Houston to spend the weekend with some high school friends. That Saturday night my friends and I went out to a bunch of parties, and I was talking about Jesus, "mightily testifying," you might say, as we drove from party to party. The beer was flowing. I would not say I was at the top of my game that night. I remember an evangelistic campaign going on at that time. Campus Crusade had plastered billboards all over town with the slogan, "I FOUND IT!" I saw one of those on the highway between one party and the next and proclaimed to the car-full of my friends, "That's me! I found it. I found Jesus." I don't believe my friends had much of an opportunity to see the truth of my proclamation that night.

At the end of the night, when my friends dropped me off at the house where I was staying, a couple of buddies had to walk me up to the door because of my inebriated condition. Thankfully, the door of the home was left open. I stumbled up the stairs to the bedroom. I'll never forget the feeling that came over me when I was alone in that room. I dropped to my knees in the darkness at the foot of the bed and wept, crying out to God to forgive me. I didn't cry and repent because I felt guilty (even though I was), I cried out to God from the depth of my understanding of His love for me and the fact that I had not reflected that love that night. That night, I identified with that "sinful woman" at the Pharisees' house. If I had been with Jesus, I too would have washed His feet with my tears, wiped them clean with whatever was available, and given Him anything I had as a gift. In that moment I knew personally and deeply the forgiveness of Christ. I returned to school with even more motivation to seek, follow, and serve Him with all my heart.

GAINING CHRIST

I love how the apostle Paul described the great driving factor of his life. Based on his experience of God's grace, seen in the book of Acts and expressed in his letters to the first-century churches, it is no surprise that Paul was so motivated to know Christ. He said,

> But whatever was to my profit I now consider loss for the sake of Christ. What is more, I consider everything a loss compared to the surpassing greatness of knowing Christ Jesus my Lord, for whose sake I have lost all things. I consider them rubbish that I may gain Christ and be found in him, not having a righteousness of my own that comes from the law, but that which is through faith in Christ — the righteousness that comes from God and is by faith. I want to know Christ and the power of his resurrection and the fellowship of sharing in his sufferings, becoming like him in his death. (Philippians 3:7-10)

Paul was set free from performance-based religion. His passion and longing for God grew out of his experience of the grace of God in Jesus Christ. We all are people who need the refreshing springs of a relationship with Christ. We are most drawn to Him and most effective when we experience His love and find Him as the rescuer of our souls and our lives.

QUESTIONS FOR REFLECTION

- Write down a list of motivations that tend to stimulate you in your spiritual life. As you look at the list, which motivations are based on performing for God or other people? Which are based on appreciation and thankfulness for what God has done?
- Make a list of all the things that you can think of that God has done for you. Pray over the list and thank Him for each one.

CHAPTER 6

WHAT THE BIBLE IS NOT

You diligently study the Scriptures because you think that by them you possess eternal life. These are the Scriptures that testify about me.

— JESUS (JOHN 5:39)

THROUGHOUT HISTORY, PEOPLE have used the Bible to create religion. The very book that was meant to bring people to God ended up being used to create rules and regulations that can actually keep us from Him! The Scriptures are God's communication to us, revealing who He is, who we are, and how we can join Him in His world-redeeming purposes. When we consider the resources available for us to pursue God and fulfill our internal longing to know Him, apart from the indwelling Holy Spirit, there is no resource greater than His communication to us in the Bible.

The Scriptures tells us that we are created for a deep and rich, lively and sustaining relationship with Christ. But those same Scriptures also provide examples of what *not* to do if we want to enjoy God and please Him fully. The religious leaders of Palestine, the Jewish big shots who controlled the religious landscape of their day, tended to major on religious observances, religious activities, or empty traditions in an attempt to earn God's favor and impress men. They were so intent on their empty code-keeping that they failed to see the miracle happening before their very eyes. On one occasion, Jesus healed a desperate invalid, but crossed the line by doing the miracle on the Sabbath, breaking one of their rules:

> When Jesus saw him lying there and learned that he had been in this condition for a long time, he asked him, "Do you want to get well?"
>
> "Sir," the invalid replied, "I have no one to help me into the pool when the water is stirred. While I am trying to get in, someone else goes down ahead of me."
>
> Then Jesus said to him, "Get up! Pick up your mat and walk." At once the man was cured; he picked up his mat and walked. (John 5:6-9)

In this spectacular account, the Scriptures reveal the character and person of God in Christ, but the religious leaders didn't get it. They started out accusing the newly mobile man, because he was carrying his mat (on which he had laid for thirty-eight years) on the Sabbath (see John 5:11-12)! Then when they discovered that it was Jesus who had done this deed on the Sabbath, they bore down on Him (see John 5:15-16). I love how *The Message* puts it: "That is why the Jews were out to get Jesus—because he did this kind of thing on the Sabbath" (verse 16).

The religious leaders of the time were so caught up with their own authority, control, and rules that they were blind to the God they were seeking to follow! The Old Testament Scriptures pointed to Jesus, but instead of seeing Him, they constructed their own religious framework and missed the main event—God Himself, come to earth and dwelling there among them. In fact, their blindness led them to persecute Jesus, not only because He did these things on the Sabbath but also because He claimed to be equal with God.

In response, Jesus didn't argue the topic at hand, but turned the discussion to the more foundational issue: These religious leaders, who prided themselves in being men of the Holy writings, did not know or understand the God they claimed to serve. He spoke of His relationship with his Father, the intimate partnership they enjoy, and the fact that those who honor the Son, honor the Father (see John 5:23).

Jesus spoke then about the importance of His Word. He reminded them of the Old Testament verses that foretold His coming and went on to communicate the importance of His words. Jesus said to the assembled religious leaders, "I tell you the truth, whoever hears my word and believes him who sent me has eternal life and will not be condemned; he has crossed over from death to life" (John 5:24).

How do you view God's Word, the Scriptures? Do you experience in them the life and benefit Jesus speaks of here?

Like the Pharisees, I was blind to God and to the true power of the Bible as a young man. I had grown up going to church periodically, but my spiritual life was one of guilt, attempted rule-keeping, and the constant feeling that I was not measuring up. Despite my religious experiences as a youth, I had never found God in His Word. When I came to faith in Christ during that freshman year of college, I suddenly had a great hunger for reading, studying, and memorizing the Bible. I was influenced by students around me who were sharing the Scriptures and letting their lives be transformed by its teaching.

In those early days of my fledgling faith, I spent much time in the Gospels, and it was almost as if I were walking those dusty Judean and Galilean roads. I met Jesus for the first time, I began to understand the heart of God, and in the process my heart was warmed and drawn toward Him. At the same time, I began to see in the person of Jesus how we are to live our lives.

If those first-century religious leaders had really been listening to and hearing the Father's heart-message in the Scriptures, they might have recognized God among them. The same principle applies today. Anyone who longs to know God would be wise to become a reader and student of God's Word, the Bible. The only way that we will escape the trap that religious people have fallen into through history — the trap of religion, blindness to the character of God, and therefore blindness to how we are to live our lives — is for us to determine to find the true God in the Bible.

That day, in His interaction over the healing of the lame man, Jesus finally brought to light the proper motivation for studying the Scriptures: "You have your heads in your Bibles constantly because you think you'll find eternal life there. But you miss the forest for the trees. These Scriptures are all about *me!*" (John 5:39, MSG). Jesus knew that the Scriptures pointed to Him.

A thorough study of the Bible reveals a single message of redemption and wholeness culminating in Jesus Christ. The Old Testament lays a foundation for the Savior of the world, whose heritage is found in the lineage of Israel and the tribe of Judah in particular. The Old Testament poetic and prophetic books point toward Him as well. The exile of the Israelites created the hope and expectancy for the One who would come to save the world and bring forgiveness of sin.

In the New Testament we have the remarkable privilege of walking with Him in the Gospels and seeing the birth of a world-changing community, the church. Through the thirty-three years of His life on earth, as well as His death and resurrection, we see that Jesus and His kingdom are the sum and meaning of everything the Bible was building up to. He is the character on whom the whole of our human drama rests — like the crowning piece of an arch, the corner posts of a building, or the center axle of a wheel. He is the one on whom all things rest and find their footing (see Colossians 1:17-18).

It is the Holy Spirit that reveals Jesus to His people as they read the Scriptures. J. M. Boice wrote,

Another result of reading the Bible is that the Holy Spirit who speaks in its pages will direct the student to Jesus. The Bible contains many varieties of material. It covers hundreds of

years of history. Still, the object of the Bible in each of its parts is to point to Jesus, and this goal is carried out on the subjective level by Christ's Spirit. Jesus said, "But when the Counselor comes, whom I shall send to you from the Father, even the Spirit of truth, who proceeds from the Father, he will bear witness to me" (John 15:26). Since the role of the Holy Spirit is to point to Jesus in the Scriptures, we can be sure that we are listening to the voice of the Holy Spirit when that happens.[1]

If we have a longing to know God and His Son more fully and intimately, we need to change our view of the Scriptures. Rather than a book of information, ideas, or rules, we see them as a love story that we are part of, an invitation to know our mighty God and to enjoy the relationship with Him that He desires.

NOT JUST WORDS ON A PAGE

One of the main reasons that any person desiring to know God more should immerse themselves in the Bible is that it is not like any other book. The biblical writers, and Jesus Christ Himself, saw the Scriptures as authoritative and alive. For that reason, we read, study, and meditate on the Bible because it is the Word of God. Two aspects that describe the power of God's Word are that it is God-breathed and is backed by God's authority.

First of all, the Bible was made alive by the inspiration of God. The apostle Paul puts it this way: "All Scripture is God-breathed and is useful for teaching, rebuking, correcting and training in righteousness, so that the man of God may be thoroughly equipped for every good work" (2 Timothy 3:16-17). Some translations use the term "inspired by God" to describe the origin of the Bible. Men and women of God can be assured that their investment in God's Word is profitable, because its words equip us for every aspect of life.

The apostle Peter, who spent years with Jesus and experienced firsthand His respect for the Word of God, described the source of Scriptures this way: "Above all, you must understand that no prophecy of Scripture came about by the prophet's own interpretation. For prophecy never had its origin in the will of man, but men spoke from God as they were carried along by the Holy Spirit" (2 Peter 1:20-21).

You see, Peter knew that the source of the biblical text was not merely human writing, but God. Basically, he is saying that the words of Scripture do not have their source in human imagination or opinion, but rather God is the impetus behind their writing. Just as a puppet is brought to life by the puppeteer, the Scriptures contain life because their author is God Himself. They are animated by God—meaning their life and power comes from the Spirit of God. Having this confidence we can be assured that the Scriptures reveal the power we need for a life of following and honoring Christ.

Secondly, it is important for us to realize that the Bible is authoritative. This is important because it sets itself apart from all other books and sets itself up as the standard by which all other ideas are judged. The writer of Hebrews clearly describes this authority: "For the word of God is living and active. Sharper than any double-edged sword, it penetrates even to dividing soul and spirit, joints and marrow; it judges the thoughts and attitudes of the heart" (Hebrews 4:12). Here again we see the description of the *life* that is resident in the Word of God. But we also get a glimpse of its authority for our life. Many times throughout the years I have experienced the power of the Bible's truth. It has the ability to penetrate to the very core of our being and it has authority to judge our thoughts and attitudes. In Psalm 19, the psalmist wrote,

> *The law of the LORD is perfect,*
> *reviving the soul.*
> *The statutes of the LORD are trustworthy,*
> *making wise the simple.*

The precepts of the LORD are right,
giving joy to the heart.
The commands of the LORD are radiant,
giving light to the eyes.
The fear of the LORD is pure,
enduring forever.
The ordinances of the LORD are sure
and altogether righteous.
They are more precious than gold,
than much pure gold;
they are sweeter than honey,
than honey from the comb.
By them is your servant warned;
in keeping them there is great reward. (verses 7-11)

The Scriptures are described as

- perfect
- trustworthy
- making wise
- right
- sure
- righteous

And then the capstone — we are warned by the words of Scripture and we experience reward in the keeping of them! The Bible has the authority of God to judge, direct, and guide our lives.

I'll never forget when as a college student, during my senior year, I was asked to lead a group of friends who were leaders in a student ministry on our campus. The first week of the new semester meant I would lead my first "leadership group" meeting with them. I was petrified. I had never led anyone in a ministry endeavor like this! On top of that, these were friends who had been followers of Christ longer than I had, whom I deeply respected and loved. A couple of days before our meeting, I remember crying out to God, asking for the words I would need to lead that group of friends. I prayed, listened, and began to write down Scripture passages that fit with what our group needed as we prepared for the new term. As God reminded me of those passages, my fears and anxiety began to cease, and I knew that I could depend on Him and His Word to be my resource for that leadership role. The meeting went very well, and we all sensed that God had met us. Because I relied on the *life* and *authority* of God's Word, I could have confidence that He had met us indeed.

When we consider the benefit that comes from engaging in the Scriptures, it is important for us to remember that they are set apart from all other literature and all other books because they find their source and their authority in God. It's been said that if the Maker of the universe and the Author of human life were to write a "recipe" to guide His children into the full abundant life He has planned, we would be wise to read it. God has written that recipe, including every spice, texture, color, and ingredient that will guarantee a life of joy, peace, and purpose—it is the Bible.

WHY LOVE THE SCRIPTURES?

We started this chapter saying that the Bible is the best and most direct source for knowing God and His Son Jesus Christ. That is the most compelling reason to engage God in the Scriptures. But four other qualities excite me and motivate me to hear, read, study, memorize, and meditate on the Word of God.

First, it is the *source of truth*. Jesus said, "I am the way and the truth and the life" (John 14:6). Truth is embodied in the person of Jesus Christ. The Scriptures reveal Him and reveal all the truth about living life. To a group of people who believed in Him, Jesus said, "If you hold to my teaching, you are really my disciples. Then you will know the truth, and the truth will set you free" (John 8:31-32).

Holding to the teaching of Christ is the way to know God and to know the truth of God. I am grateful to God for the spiritual mentors over the years that have directed me to the Scriptures and pointed out the truth for life found in them.

Second, it is the *source of spiritual nourishment.* Job said, "I have not departed from the commands of his lips; I have treasured the words of his mouth more than my daily bread" (Job 23:12). And the psalmist put it this way, "How sweet are your words to my taste, sweeter than honey to my mouth!" (Psalm 119:103). In times of celebration, in times of distress, and every time in between, God's Word has nourished my soul.

Third, it provides *wisdom and guidance for life.* The Proverbs give a consistent drumbeat of this message:

> *My son, if you accept my words*
> *and store up my commands within you,*
> *turning your ear to wisdom*
> *and applying your heart to understanding,*
> *and if you call out for insight*
> *and cry aloud for understanding,*
> *and if you look for it as for silver*
> *and search for it as for hidden treasure,*
> *then you will understand the fear of the* LORD
> *and find the knowledge of God.*
> *For the* LORD *gives wisdom,*
> *and from his mouth come knowledge and understanding.*
> (Proverbs 2:1-6)

The psalmist poetically expressed the same longing and truth, "Your word is a lamp to my feet and a light for my path" (Psalm 119:105). There have been many times in my life when I didn't know how to respond or which way to go. His words have given guidance and direction, especially for living in the way He has designed us to live.

Fourth, God's Word is a *primary resource for those who join Him in His kingdom work.* Each of us has the opportunity to reflect the Christ-life before a watching world, to communicate the good news of Christ in word and deed, to help others grow spiritually, and to bring kingdom righteousness and justice into the darkness of an often hopeless world. The apostle Paul knew what it took to be a kingdom worker. Near the end of his life, in a letter to Timothy, his son in the faith, he said, "Do your best to present yourself to God as one approved, a workman who does not need to be ashamed and who correctly handles the word of truth" (2 Timothy 2:15). The landscape of their time was filled with false teaching and heresy. The only way that a man or woman who desires to have an impact in our world can be sure of his or her teaching is if it is grounded in the Word of God.

Do you want to be used in the lives of others for Christ's sake? The one who will have confidence as a worker for the kingdom is the person who correctly handles the Scriptures. Leroy Eims, one of the pioneers of The Navigators' collegiate ministry, is quoted as saying, "If you become a master of God's Word, you will never be out of a job!" People who know the Scriptures will always be pursued because the Scriptures are the source of life and wisdom. Over the years, God has provided various opportunities for me to serve Him. In most cases I found myself in over my head. Each step along the way, my time in the Scriptures has drawn me to Jesus and pointed me to the resources He alone can provide for life.

GOD'S WORD IN THE DESERT

During Israel's forty years in the wilderness of Sinai after they were released from Egyptian captivity, Moses was constantly challenged as he led the people. As is often the case in our own lives, the harder the journey became, the more he wanted to know God. At one juncture, God told Moses that He would be with him (see Exodus 33:14). But Moses wanted more, he wanted a fuller manifestation of knowing

God (see Exodus 33:18). God answered Moses' request and offered to meet him. But when the time came for God's glory to be more fully revealed to Moses, God spoke His Word to him:

> Then the LORD came down in the cloud and stood there with him and proclaimed his name, the LORD. And he passed in front of Moses, proclaiming, "The LORD, the LORD, the compassionate and gracious God, slow to anger, abounding in love and faithfulness, maintaining love to thousands, and forgiving wickedness, rebellion and sin." (Exodus 34:5-7)

God went way beyond a flashy display for Moses, He gave him words from His lips that Moses could take with him on the wilderness trails and share with his countrymen as well. Do you have a longing to know God? Become one who hears, reads, studies, memorizes, and meditates on His words. (See appendix A for a helpful illustration.) Men and women throughout the ages have found that the Word of God is a powerful, living source of knowing Him and His Son Jesus Christ.

QUESTIONS FOR REFLECTION

- After reading this chapter, what new things have you learned about the Bible and about the impact the Word of God can have on your life?
- Is there a *new* way that you can include the Scriptures in your life—hearing, reading, studying, memorizing, meditating—that you could begin this week?

CHAPTER 7

FINDING GOD IN PRAYER AND HIS PROMISES

The function of the prayer of faith is to turn God's promises into facts of experience.

— J. O. SANDERS

I WAS IN the seventh grade, need I say more? Any stereotypes one might have regarding junior high males will serve pretty accurately. My spiritual condition was no different from that of my peers. I had little idea of God's love for me; my relationship with Christ was limited to a little pinch of guilt that kept me showing up for Sunday services. I was much more interested in baseball.

I played second base on a team called the Tigers. Our Little League team was regarded as decent in Chicago's suburban hinterlands where we lived and played, but one formidable obstacle stood between our team and the area league championship. That was the White Sox, a dynasty of near mythic proportions coached by none other than Old Man Selmiski. Selmiski farmed mink just north of town and the rumor was that he fed his boys and his mink the same magic potion. Because of it, the White Sox grew faster and sleeker than the rest of us.

As the season progressed, my desire to beat the White Sox grew to an obsession. So far, our team was doing okay with six wins and three losses, but we were certainly not bound for the play-offs. The White Sox, on the other hand, were undefeated as always. The early May night before we were slated to play them I couldn't sleep. I was fixed on what it would be like to beat Selmiski's boys. I lay in bed imagining myself achieving heroic feats, hitting home runs, diving for ground balls, closing my glove around a game-winning catch. Then I knelt at the foot of my bed for a serious conversation with God. I don't remember exactly what I prayed, but I know I firmly believed that God could pull off a win for the Tigers.

The next day as we went through pre-game warm-ups, we trembled to realize that each of the Sox players was at least a head taller than any of us, a stat certainly due to the team's regular intake of some elixir of mink urine and rodent parts. But then, as the game unfolded, we watched the scoreboard awestruck. First, the Tigers pulled close in runs. Then an outright miracle occurred. We won. The Tigers beat those White Sox, 4 to 3. If we'd been big enough to pull down the backstop it would have been toppled by a swarm of Tigers. While the 1980 U.S. Olympic hockey victory over the Russians was a historic victory, for our team of underdog thirteen-year-old boys this win was every bit as meaningful. As I rejoiced with my buddies, I remembered my foot-of-the-bed prayer the night before. Without a doubt I knew that God had answered that prayer.

GETTING TO THE HEART OF PRAYER

When I think back on that young ball player and his audacious prayers, my first response is to wince. Isn't it immature and shallow to pray to win a Little League ball game? The more I think about it, though, I'm not so sure. As an adult, I still believe that win took some divine intervention. Who am I to question whether the God of the universe could grant a young boy's barely-believing prayer? Perhaps

He did it in order to draw me closer to knowing Him. That, after all, is a key element of prayer—connecting His children with Himself in authentic dependence. As we learn about God's character and the purpose of prayer in the Bible, we enter into that relationship more deeply. Jesus uses a parable to teach His disciples how prayer reveals both the heart of the one who prays and the heart of the God who hears those prayers (see Luke 18).

Jesus chooses the plight of a widow cruelly oppressed by an adversary as His subject in this parable. She goes to a judge appointed to bring justice for people, but this judge ignores her. As we consider the vulnerability and need of this woman, we are indignant and distraught at the widow's pain and angry at the indifference of the judge.

Finally, she experiences a breakthrough. Jesus describes the judge's response to the woman's persistent pleas: "For some time he refused. But finally he said to himself, 'Even though I don't fear God or care about men, yet because this widow keeps bothering me, I will see that she gets justice, so that she won't eventually wear me out with her coming!'" (Luke 18:4-5).

Over time, through the widow's repetitive "bothering," the heart of the judge changed. In the end the widow got results. Our heavenly Father is not like that; Jesus said, "Listen to what the unjust judge says. And will not God bring about justice for his chosen ones, who cry out to him day and night? Will he keep putting them off? I tell you, he will see that they get justice, and quickly" (Luke 18:6-8).

Our heavenly Father is a God who hears, a God who brings justice. As we become people of prayer, we will learn that God is not indifferent. We don't have to edit our prayers or worry that our requests are too basic or that they don't conform to some kind of pious standard. Just as a loving earthly father does not expect his children to filter their requests, we aren't called to filter the list we submit to God. God will prioritize our list for us, as He knows our most urgent needs. He will not keep putting us off. Rather, He will act on our behalf. God longs to bring help to those who cry out to Him (see Luke 11:9-13), and His care for His children is generous. We can trust that God's goodness and generosity will be reflected in His responses to all our prayers, big and small (see Matthew 10:29-31).

Jesus also teaches in this parable that our prayers reveal much about us. The widow did not give up. She's our model. Believing what Scripture teaches—that we have a heavenly Father who compassionately hears and acts on our behalf—we are to persevere as she persevered, bringing all our needs to Him. As we seek God humbly, mindful of our condition as broken and weak human beings, He is faithful (see Hebrews 10:23) to respond and we will grow in faith, ever learning of His goodness and readiness to help us.

Just as in the case with the widow, sometimes the answers to my prayers haven't come quite as quickly as those I saw as a Tiger second baseman. Pam and I went through a season of ministry when the leadership skills I was expected to demonstrate were severely challenged. I had to make significant personnel changes. Although I did this with prayer and after seeking the counsel of many, the changes meant painful loss for a number of people. My heart was heavy as I moved forward with various decisions. Conflict with others caused me to feel hurt, betrayed, discouraged, and anxious. Those feelings were compounded by a tendency I've described before, an overly sensitive desire to perform and to please.

Pam and I felt we were under assault by circumstances and people beyond our control. Those were dark days, but they yielded some good fruit. During that time I was constantly driven to my knees and longed for a sense of peace and release from conflict. God eventually granted those pleas, to a certain extent. First, however, He used this struggling time to bring me to the end of myself. Through that time and many since, I'm learning that a deepening prayer life is a lifelong pursuit well worth the effort. Prayer can open whole new vistas of relationship with God, even as our earthly life becomes crowded with difficulties. As I get to know Him more intimately in the depths of my soul, I learn more about who He is and I learn, sometimes kicking and screaming, more about myself.

PRAYING THE PROMISES OF GOD

One activity of prayer that has been a foundation for many believers as they have pressed into God's presence over the centuries is attention to the promises He makes in the Scriptures. God's Word is filled with His promises to His people and to each individual who puts his or her trust in Him. Peter speaks of the power and blessing the promises are to those of us in Christ,

> *His divine power has given us everything we need for life and godliness through our knowledge of him who called us by his own glory and goodness. Through these he has given us his very great and precious promises, so that through them you may participate in the divine nature and escape the corruption in the world caused by evil desires.* (2 Peter 1:3-4)

J. I. Packer, in his classic *Knowing God*, says,

> *In the days when the Bible was universally acknowledged in the churches as "God's Word written," it was clearly understood that the promises of God recorded in Scripture were the proper, God-given basis for all our life of faith, and that the way to strengthen one's faith was to focus it upon particular promises that spoke to one's condition.*[1]

There are two types of promises found in Scripture: general and specific. General promises are given to all God's people and they come with no expiration date. They express God's intentions for all His people in all places and at all times. The most familiar is perhaps John 3:16, a general promise for each follower of Christ: "For God so loved the world that he gave his one and only Son, that whoever believes in him shall not perish but have eternal life."

Paul also speaks of general promises available to all those who are in Christ.

For the Son of God, Jesus Christ, who was preached among you by me and Silas and Timothy, was not "Yes" and "No," but in him it has always been "Yes." For no matter how many promises God has made, they are "Yes" in Christ. And so through him the "Amen" is spoken by us to the glory of God. (2 Corinthians 1:19-20)

Other specific promises are given to specific people for specific times. For instance, God told Moses that he would take the people of Israel out of the oppressive hand of Pharaoh and bring them to the Promised Land (see Exodus 3). Another example is when He told David to go and attack the Philistines in Keilah, promising victory (see 1 Samuel 23:1-6). There are many examples of God making specific promises to His people. God may impress upon us through the Scriptures and by the Holy Spirit an assurance of some kind for which we are to trust Him.

During our years of ministry in Lawrence, Kansas, Pam and I had large groups of university students into our home on a regular basis. During one season of ministry, our home was frequently packed to overflowing. We were delighted with God's blessing, but the crowding began to affect our family life. Pam and I felt impressed that just as David was given the promise of a house (temple) that would be built for the glory of God (see 2 Samuel 7), we also were called to pray and ask God to do the same for us. We didn't tell anyone, but began to pray that God would move in a clear way to provide funds to allow us to get into a house that would hold the large number of students attending our ministry meetings. We started, by faith, looking for a new house. When realtors would ask about our finances and how we could afford a specific house, we told them that we had confidence that God would provide. As we searched and prayed we found that we would need an additional $40,000 to get into the kind of house we would need for our ministry groups.

A few months after we began praying, we received a phone call from a friend asking if there was anything in particular that we had need for or anything we had been praying about in regards to our family or ministry. He went on to say that he had a significant gift he was considering giving. By the end of that conversation he had promised $20,000 to our new home. Later that week, we were talking with another friend and supporter of our ministry. They asked a similar question regarding our finances. Feeling prompted by God, we shared with her how we had sensed God leading us. That day she committed $20,000 to fulfill our needs. All in a week's time, without writing any letters or organizing any campaigns, God answered our prayers for the building of "a house for His Name." Several months later we moved into that house. Soon it too was filled to overflowing with students who were hungry for God and His Word.

Tom Yeakley, a national and international leader with The Navigators, has written a very helpful book called *Praying over God's Promises*. Some of my thoughts in this chapter come from his book and his counsel over the years. He gives good guidance to our praying over promise verses and passages that are motivational for us,

General and specific promises are given to believers for guidance and encouragement. Though general promises are many, specific promises are few. We should not expect to have specific promises given to us very often and when we do find one, we must be certain that it is God speaking to us. A key is to have an attitude of expectancy as we approach the Scriptures, longing to meet with God and to hear His voice, and expecting to fellowship with Him through His Word. Most of the time, we will find encouragement and comfort from the

general promises in the Word. But occasionally, the Lord will
impress upon our hearts some passages of Scripture that will
be very specific to our current situation or need. These special
promises are to be believed and acted upon.[2]

The list of men and women of faith who believed that God's promises were for them and gave themselves in prayer over the promises of God is long and noteworthy. Some of the names you might recognize are Martin Luther, Hudson Taylor, Amy Carmichael, J. O. Fraser, D. L. Moody, Elisabeth Elliot, and Dawson Trotman. J. O. Sanders spoke of the place of prayer as we consider the promises of God,

But promises must be distinguished from facts. We accept a
stated fact of God's Word, but we plead a promise. When God
proclaims a fact, faith accepts and acts upon it. When God
makes a promise, we comply with its conditions, claim its ful-
fillment and receive the promised favor. The function of the
prayer of faith is to turn God's promises into facts of experi-
ence. The patriarchs through faith obtained the fulfillment of
God's promises (Hebrews 11:33), and turned them into per-
sonal experience.[3]

GOD'S ANSWERS SUSTAIN US

Remember those challenging, conflict-filled days I mentioned earlier? During those many dark nights when I'd awaken crying out to Him, He did provide help. His grace sustained us with timely promises and answers to prayer to sustain us on the journey. These are a few of the specific lifesaving truths that carried us through that difficult season:

- I am your strength! "I love you, O LORD, my strength. The
  LORD is my rock, my fortress and my deliverer; my God is my

rock, in whom I take refuge. He is my shield and the horn of my salvation, my stronghold" (Psalm 18:1-2).

- I am with you and delight and rejoice in you! "The LORD your God is with you, he is mighty to save. He will take great delight in you, he will quiet you with his love, he will rejoice over you with singing" (Zephaniah 3:17).
- I walk with you through the challenges! "For I am the LORD, your God, who takes hold of your right hand and says to you, Do not fear; I will help you" (Isaiah 41:13).

There is no question that in order to become a person of influence for God's kingdom, we must first become people who long for God and find rich relationship with Him through prayer. As we appeal to God for His help, His guidance, and His protection, we learn more about Him and about ourselves. We also bring before Him the promises He has made in His Word. As we walk with Him in prayer, we come to know Him more deeply, and the refreshing, abundant life He gives us overflows to others.

QUESTIONS FOR REFLECTION

- Describe your prayer life in a sentence or two. What does it tell you about your view of God and your view of yourself?
- Are there any promises from the Bible that act as a foundation for your life? What are they? If not, consider reading the Psalms or Isaiah 40–66 and ask God to give you a promise about who He is or what He will do as you trust Him.

CHAPTER 8

INTO HIS IMAGE

Every Christian is to become a little Christ. The whole purpose of becoming a Christian is simply nothing else.

— C. S. LEWIS

APPARENTLY PAM AND I thought we were superheroes when we accepted a position with Doulos Ministries in Lawrence, Kansas, in 1990. In addition to ministering to local junior high, senior high, and college students, our job required that we put in a full workweek plus several evenings a week in ministry activity, recruit five to ten recent college graduates to join us full-time in ministry, and raise $150,000 to support the ministry. The commute wasn't bad, because the office for the ministry was located in our basement, but the stress of the work became overwhelming. Oh, yeah, and did I mention that we had three children under six years old at that time?

On one particular evening, we had a large group of people coming over for dinner. As we were getting ready for their arrival, Pam and I got into an argument. At the same time, the kids were having a meltdown—whining, crying, and basically being kids. I was stressed and impatient, and I lost my cool with Pam and yelled at the kids. I retreated to our bedroom to get ready for the group that was about to descend on our home. As I changed clothes, I happened to look into the mirror. As I looked at my face staring back at me, my mind was full of questions: *Am I becoming the kind of husband and father that I swore I would never be? Am I making any progress at all as a follower of Jesus? Isn't the power of Jesus supposed to change me? Does the Christian life really work?*

It is in moments like these, when we're overcome and harried with life, that God often stops us and brings us to a point of reckoning. God doesn't want us to lead superficial, unexamined lives. Instead, He wants us to know ourselves honestly and realize that we are entirely dependent on Him every hour. And it is so important for us to understand the final goal of our desire and yearning for God. As we long for God and pursue Him, even at our lowest moments, He is committed to grow each of us into a person who reflects His character.

BE PERFECT?

As we've discussed earlier, the religious leaders of Jesus' day were more interested in ritual than in relationship. Their spirituality had little to do with knowing God and becoming like Him. Sadly, that tendency toward legalism and superficial piety remains a common substitute for life-giving faith today. It's good to be reminded that throughout His ministry Jesus worked to expose the emptiness of religious rituals devoid of changed hearts and new lives. In the Sermon on the Mount, Jesus challenged His listeners and His disciples, saying, "For I tell you that unless your righteousness surpasses that of the Pharisees and the teachers of the law, you will certainly not enter the kingdom of heaven" (Matthew 5:20). Moments later, He set the bar even higher commanding them simply, "Be perfect, therefore, as your heavenly Father is perfect" (Matthew 5:48).

Jesus has a clear agenda for the lives of His followers—radical transformation—and He doesn't keep it hidden. In the Beatitudes, Christ says, "Blessed are those who hunger and thirst for righteousness, for they will be filled" (Matthew 5:6). Jesus desires for our lives to be characterized by a deep longing for God and His powerful life-changing presence. There is nothing in such a life of kingdom living to be confused with dry and dreary legalistic religiosity. This is a life the Pharisees couldn't even dream of, because it's only possible through Christ.

That day, as I looked in the mirror and longed for myself to be "better" and to experience change that would serve my wife and my family, God was already on the job. It was early in the first inning, perhaps, but the game change had begun. I was beginning to experience the hunger God created me to suffer, the longing for His presence and priorities in my life. That's the hunger Jesus blesses, the same painful gnawing that He promises to satisfy with His presence.

DIVINELY DESIGNED MIRRORS

Did you ever experience the "mirror room" in the fun house at the carnival or country fair? It's a very entertaining room, filled with mirrors that manipulate your image. If you are short, there's a mirror that makes you stretch to the height of an NBA post-man. If you are a bit overweight and wanting to regain that hour-glass figure, no problem, one of the mirrors can take off twenty pounds! When you position yourself correctly, another mirror can make your upper body look like pro wrestler turned movie star Dwayne Johnson, "The Rock." As fun as that room is, as soon as you leave, you are back where you started. It is encouraging to know that God not only has a plan for the permanent renovation of our character, but also for our image problems. And He reveals it from the earliest pages of the Bible:

> Then God said, "Let us make man in our image, in our likeness, and let them rule over the fish of the sea and the birds of the air, over the livestock, over all the earth, and over all the creatures that move along the ground."
> So God created man in his own image, in the image of God he created him; male and female he created them.

God blessed them and said to them, "Be fruitful and increase in number; fill the earth and subdue it." (Genesis 1:26-28)

From Genesis on, our Father never wavers. God's purpose and plan for humankind is that we reflect His image, that we be *imago dei*—the image of God. Anthony Hoekema, in his book *Created in God's Image*, says that humanity is to *mirror* God: "When one looks at a human being, one ought to see in him or her a certain reflection of God. Another way of putting this is to say that in man God is to become visible on earth." Further, Hoekema says man is to *represent* God. God's desire for His creation is that men and women be constant reminders and representatives of His own likeness and character.[1]

Walter Brueggemann, in his commentary on Genesis, points out an interesting irony. Although the Israelites were to have no images (see Exodus 20:4) before them, God created man and woman in His own image. In doing so people will always have His image in human form before them.[2] Throughout history it has been common for kings to erect statues throughout their realms reminding subjects who is in charge. *Imago dei* reflects this same idea. God's image is meant to be represented everywhere through us, reminding us that He is our reigning king.

God's first commission to man is to be "be fruitful and increase in number; fill the earth and subdue it." Through the means of child-bearing, men and women increase the number of reflections of God inhabiting the earth. Not only did God create each of us as His own mirror to reflect His character, He orders the generational production of more and more mirrors to reflect His never-changing likeness—the perfect image of goodness, justice, mercy, and holiness.

DEAD MEN WALKING

So you say, "Doug, maybe you're right. God may have made us to pursue and to reflect Him, but the world is such a mess! How can

God's vision for generations reflecting His perfect character ever be realized?"

The fact that a relationship with God forms the foundation for a radically changed life is great news for a planet filled with men and women caught in the cascading challenge of generational brokenness and sin. The apostle Paul writes to the church at Ephesus, "As for you, you were dead in your transgressions and sins, in which you used to live when you followed the ways of this world and of the ruler of the kingdom of the air, the spirit who is now at work in those who are disobedient" (Ephesians 2:1-2).

Paul says that we live in a world of dead men walking. These words conjure scenes from cheesy old horror movies such as *Night of the Living Dead*. Remember the dead rising stiff-legged from their graves and strolling down the sidewalks to terrify the unsuspecting town folk? The spiritual reality is that before a person comes in contact with Jesus and experiences the miracle of new spiritual birth, he or she is just such a walking corpse. Each of us has been among the walking dead. In Genesis 2:17, God warned of this fate when He laid out the boundaries in Eden: "You must not eat from the tree of the knowledge of good and evil, for when you eat of it you will surely die." Sure enough, Adam and Eve munched that irresistible fruit. Their sin left death in its wake.

As believers, we can callously and casually talk about spiritual death, but the reality of being dead men walking is quite a grave situation. Let's do an autopsy on the status of a spiritual corpse. As we look at the facts, we can have a renewed clarity regarding our past life and an immense gratitude for what God has done and is doing to set us free. Before Christ redeemed us, we were

- Separated from relationship with God (see Genesis 3:23-24)
- Enslaved by desires not pleasing to God (see Ephesians 2:3)
- Lacking lasting hope (see Ephesians 2:12)
- Citizens and disciples of the kingdom of darkness (see Colossians 1:13)

- Damaged in our relationship with others (see Ephesians 2:14-19)
- Spiritually blind and foolish (see 2 Corinthians 4:4 and Romans 1:21,28)
- Deserving and destined for God's judgment (see Ephesians 2:3)

THE GOOD INFECTION

I am amazed and frequently grateful to the point of tears when I recognize God's ongoing redeeming rescue in my life. In 2 Corinthians 3 we hear of God's desire to set us free from the captivity of sin that spiritual death represents and to restore us completely to reflect His image:

> *Now, the Lord is the Spirit, and wherever the Spirit of the Lord is, he gives freedom. And all of us have had that veil removed so that we can be mirrors that brightly reflect the glory of the Lord. And as the Spirit of the Lord works within us, we become more and more like him and reflect his glory even more.* (verses 17-18, NLT)

Our longings for and pursuit of God take us straight into His purposes for us. As we seek Him, over time, we become like Him. In Romans, the apostle Paul speaks of God's purposes in all the events of our lives:

> *And we know that God causes everything to work together for the good of those who love God and are called according to his purpose for them. For God knew his people in advance, and he chose them to become like his Son, so that his Son would be the firstborn, with many brothers and sisters.* (8:28-29, NLT)

Jesus Christ came to earth, God in human flesh, to show us what God is like, and to rescue us through His death and resurrection.

Our destiny is to become like Jesus. In another letter, Paul speaks of his own passion for the Galatian church. He feels as though he is in the pains of childbirth "until Christ's life becomes visible" in the lives of those dear Galatian friends (Galatians 4:19, MSG).

C. S. Lewis put it this way:

> Now the whole offer which Christianity makes is this: that we can, if we let God have His way, come to share in the life of Christ. If we do, we shall then be sharing a life which was begotten, not made, which always has existed and always will exist. Christ is the Son of God. If we share in this kind of life we also shall be sons of God. We shall love the Father as He does and the Holy Ghost will arise in us. He came to this world and became a man in order to spread to other men the kind of life He has — by what I call "good infection." Every Christian is to become a little Christ. The whole purpose of becoming a Christian is simply nothing else.[3]

Part 4, "Na Pali Coast," will have more to say regarding the transformation that God desires for our lives. In part 2 we've focused on an important attribute that characterizes people God empowers to influence and change our world. Jesus says it all succinctly and powerfully: "Live in me. Make your home in me just as I do in you. In the same way that a branch can't bear grapes by itself but only by being joined to the vine, you can't bear fruit unless you are joined with me" (John 15:4, MSG).

A relationship with the Creator of the universe, the King of kings, is deeply motivated by His gracious love. It is energized by a keen awareness of all God has done for us. Our longing for God finds its greatest satisfaction as we pursue Him in the Scriptures, the inspired Word of God. The lifeblood of our relationship with God is prayerful communication and faith in His promises. Our hope and our longing is to become more and more like Jesus. In His hands and by His Spirit we are transformed, we become useful to Him, we become world changers and world influencers.

However, our relationship with God and a life lived for Him is not designed to be lived alone, but rather in a divine connection with others on the journey. In the next section we will see the environment in which life in Jesus is designed to operate—the ecosystem of the spiritual life—a community of friends we'll call the Coral Reef!

QUESTIONS FOR REFLECTION

- Name an area of your character or a pattern in your life that you would like to see more fully reflect the character of God. Pray and ask God to begin changing you so that you become increasingly more like Jesus in that area.
- Look at the list of descriptions in the section called "Dead Men Walking" that portray people without Christ. Do any of these areas still describe aspects of your life? Pray for God's help.

PART 3

THE CORAL REEF

Where We Find Our Place in God's Vast and
Wonderful Spiritual Ecosystem

CHAPTER 9

COMMUNITY: GOD'S DESIGN FOR LIFE

Before Jesus' death and resurrection and after His death and resurrection, what was He doing? He was creating a community.

— TIM KELLER

ON AN ANNIVERSARY trip, Pam and I got a chance to snorkel in Hawaii. We had read up on all the best reefs to explore, rented our gear, and drove to the beach to get ready. I had read somewhere in a tourist magazine about getting some fish food to entice the fish. I bought a couple little packets at the scuba shop where we rented our equipment. We began to paddle our way offshore and it wasn't long before we began to see some fish. I thought, *I bet if I sprinkle a little fish food in the water it will coax a few more out of hiding!* As I treaded water, I pulled one of the packets out of my pocket and tried to make a small tear in the bag. As I did so, a large, aggressive fish—that had obviously seen one of those bags of food before—darted up and ripped off the top of the bag, spilling a cloud of fish food into the water. Suddenly I was engulfed in a fish frenzy, flocked by fish of every color, size, and shape.

Needless to say, that day Pam and I got to know "up close and personally" many of the varied personalities and characters who lived in the community known as the coral reef. We marveled as the waves and surf brought food and nourishment to the anemones and urchins. I love the dancing action of the anemones and sea vegetation. We saw clown fish who serve the anemones by cleaning them, despite their poisonous tentacles. We saw moray eels, hidden in the cracks of the reef, ready to ambush an unsuspecting passerby. A reef shark swam through the deep passageways looking for a lobster or crab, while above it a sea turtle swam past as if flying through the watery turbulence. Fish, animals, and plant life of every imaginable kind lived in a collaborative living environment, some cleaning and serving others in a symbiotic symphony only God could have dreamed up.

In the last chapter we talked of the spiritual death that only the gospel can overcome. One symptom of spiritual death is seen in humans' inclination toward relational estrangement. Gilbert Bilezikian, in his book *Community 101*, says, "Not only did sin separate humans from God, it also separated them from each other."[1] One result of the sin and brokenness in our world is the loss of life-giving community, such as we see so vividly in God's creation. Just as fish in the reef that try to go it alone are susceptible to enemies lurking in the depths, so many followers of Jesus today are vulnerable when they live in isolation, devoid of authentic and meaningful relationships and so ignoring the design of God.

For some, that isolation isn't literal—many of the loneliest people I see are awash in a sea of acquaintances. We all know that authentic community doesn't necessarily come in a crowd. The community God intends is deep more often than wide. God's Word is full of examples (see Acts 2:42-47), prayers (see John 17:21,23), and admonitions (see Hebrews 10:24-25) for God's people to come together in community. God also makes it clear that He longs for our experience of community to mirror the love for others that Christ modeled (see John 13:34-35) and for us to find our place in a local expression of the church—the fullest and most powerful expression of community as believers (see Ephesians 1:22-23).

USA Today recently reported that "Americans have a third fewer close friends and confidants then just two decades ago—a sign that people may be living lonelier, more isolated lives."[2] Our world is desperately wanting and needing the kind of life that God has designed us to live—one filled with deep, life-giving relationships drawn from the kind of life He alone gives. When we consider the kind of community that reflects God's design and develops us as His people, we can also imagine the powerful influence that kind of life-giving community can have when lived out among those without the hope we have in Christ.

WHERE COMMUNITY BEGAN

Adam and Eve were the first community God designed. God had made Adam, and in Genesis 2:18, declared that "It is not good for the man to be alone. I will make a helper suitable for him"—a companion. After gathering all the animals to Adam, God saw that none of them were adequate companions:

> But for Adam no suitable helper was found. So the LORD God caused the man to fall into a deep sleep; and while he was sleeping, he took one of the man's ribs and closed up the place with flesh. Then the LORD God made a woman from the rib he had taken out of the man, and he brought her to the man.
> The man said,
>
> "This is now bone of my bones
>   and flesh of my flesh;
> she shall be called 'woman,'
>   for she was taken out of man."
>
> For this reason a man will leave his father and mother and be united to his wife, and they will become one flesh.
> The man and his wife were both naked, and they felt no shame. (Genesis 2:20-25)

God's creation of Eve brought into being the full expression of the image of God, male and female. In their case, this relationship was unfettered in their pre-sin state of existence. Adam and Eve reflected the image of God, so the mandate to "be fruitful and increase in number" (Genesis 1:28) would by design multiply the image of God. Not only did Adam and Eve, that first community, reflect the communal nature of God, but in addition they were given the mandate to "fill the earth and subdue it." Humans were given responsibility and a mission that would depend on their obedience. Community was always God's "plan A" for mankind. It was never good for them to be alone.

A KINGDOM FAMILY

Not long after the creation of the first family the earth was filled with them. But not all of them were living as God intended, in relationship with Him. Called out from among the nations, in Israel we see God's intent to create a family who, over a number of generations, would become His own nation. Regarding the call to Abraham in Genesis 12:1-3, Walter Brueggemann says, "The first call of God is in calling the worlds into being, the work of creation. In this second call, God calls an alternative community, an alternative to the cold, barren ones who have ceased to listen and have therefore ceased to live and ceased to hope."[3]

In Exodus 19:4-6, we see God's words that communicate the identity and blessing that was supposed to characterize this "alternative community," the nation of Israel:

> *You yourselves have seen what I did to Egypt, and how I carried you on eagles' wings and brought you to myself. Now if you obey me fully and keep my covenant, then out of all nations you will be my treasured possession. Although the whole earth is mine, you will be for me a kingdom of priests and a holy nation.*

Here we see the promise to these people of communion with God as His "treasured possession" and their mission as a "kingdom of priests" and a "holy nation." J. I. Durham, in his commentary on Exodus, points out that "they are to be a people set apart, different from all other people by what they are, and are becoming—a display-people, a showcase to the world of how being in covenant with Yahweh changes a people."[4]

Here we see both the relational and missional dimensions of community. Israel existed as God's special possession and was promised a special relationship with Him. Out of that relationship with God they would be a blessing to the nations. They were positioned and empowered by God to make waves of grace that flow out to the surrounding nations.

COME, FOLLOW ME

Perhaps we see God's heart for community most strikingly in the group of disciples that followed Jesus. A. B. Bruce says, "From the evangelic records it appears that Jesus began at a very early period of His ministry to gather round Him a company of disciples, with a view to the preparation of an agency for carrying on the work of the divine kingdom.[5] How often do we consider this important aspect of Christ's work?

Tim Keller makes it even clearer: "Before Jesus' death and resurrection and after His death and resurrection, what was He doing? You say, 'He was teaching and preaching.' Yes, but what was He doing? He was creating a community."[6] In Mark 1:17, Jesus said to those who would follow Him, "Come, follow me . . . and I will make you fishers of men." They were called at once to both relationship and purpose. Their mission together created the context for a growing community, and their community was the soil from which their mission grew. Mark 3:13-15 describes the calling of the apostles: "Jesus went up on a mountainside and called to him those he wanted, and they came to him. He appointed twelve—designating them apostles—that they might be with him and that he might send them out to preach and to have authority to drive out demons."

To be with Him and to be sent out, that was the community Jesus prescribed.

LIVING STONES

Finally, we see God's heart and design for community evidenced in the birthing of the early church. Peter describes God's chosen identity for the church in the New Testament, which bears resemblance to the characteristics God placed upon Israel.

> *As you come to him, the living Stone — rejected by men but chosen by God and precious to him — you also, like living stones, are being built into a spiritual house to be a holy priesthood, offering spiritual sacrifices acceptable to God through Jesus Christ. . . .*
>
> *But you are a chosen people, a royal priesthood, a holy nation, a people belonging to God, that you may declare the praises of him who called you out of darkness into his wonderful light.* (1 Peter 2:4-5,9)

Peter Davids comments on verse 5, describing the community of believers as "living stones": "These are not individual stones, but a collective group as part of God's temple, formed into a 'spiritual house,' meaning it is the Spirit who forms it. In addition, this is not a physical building, but a living, spiritual house."[7] The term "house" (*oikos*) is used throughout the New Testament and speaks of both a literal household and also a metaphor for community in Christ. These words are rich with the invitation of God into a special relationship: chosen and joined with Christ, a priesthood that belongs to the King, holy (set apart) as special to God, and a people belonging to God.

In this passage, we see the church living out the purposes of God by announcing the glorious deeds of God. These deeds of God include creation and all His gracious saving actions, including the redemption we have in Christ. The church's common purpose continues in verse 12 where they are called to "Live such good lives among the pagans that, though they accuse you of doing wrong, they may see your good deeds and glorify God on the day he visits us." Thriving—not just surviving—in the world, the church brings glory to God in just the way that He intended.

STANDARD EQUIPMENT

In the creation of Adam and Eve, the nation of Israel, the disciples of Christ, and His design for the church in the present day, we see God's heart for community as He intends. We are to live in connection with God and others, serving God and His purposes. God-designed community is both *relational*, putting us together in caring, authentic, dependent relationships; and *missional*, bonding us together with others who are about God's desires.

So, what is the "standard equipment" God has identified that will enable us to live in community that is both relational and missional? I have spent the past couple of years searching the Scriptures and talking with many individuals and groups, seeking to learn more about the essential ingredients God desires. There seem to be five essentials that distinguish the community that God intends—interdependence, vulnerable authenticity, life transformation, the mission of God, and whole-life worship. These topics will be addressed in the rest of part 3.

QUESTIONS FOR REFLECTION

• What do you think causes people in our society to live such independent lives?

- On a scale from 1–10, rate how you currently feel that you are experiencing community with other people. What makes you feel that way?
- Who are some people that you could get closer to and grow with as followers of Jesus? Pray for God's help to increase your experience of community.

CHAPTER 10

LIVING IN INTERDEPENDENCE

God is calling together little communities of the heart to fight for one another and for the hearts of those who have not yet been set free.

— JOHN ELDREDGE

DURING A MISSION trip to the island of Sumatra in Indonesia several members of our team, along with a local missionary, Bruce, decided to take a weekend break to travel a couple of hours away and climb the long dormant Mount Merapi. Although a tourist magazine urged us to "Climb Mount Merapi, feel the ground rumble beneath your feet," local guides told us the crater had not experienced any eruptive activity in sixteen years.

After leaving our car in the small West Sumatran village of Bukittinggi, we climbed the southern slope of Mount Merapi, where we joined a community of locals who had spent the night camping. As our growing band of hikers progressed up the slope, we met numerous groups of Indonesian students eager to share in the picture taking and in the general celebratory enthusiasm of this holiday excursion to view the volcanic crater. We were told we had about a three-hour walk ahead. Along the way we enjoyed chatting with those we met on the path, overcoming the language barriers, and exchanging recommendations for awesome photo ops of the shimmering landscapes stretching from the Indian Ocean to the inland rice and banana plantations.

As our group of four walked around the nearly mile-wide volcanic pit, we paused frequently to peer into the seemingly bottomless crater. Then, just as we began to walk away to begin our descent, the nightmare began. An explosion boomed from deep within the volcano's heart. After sixteen years of relative silence, Mount Merapi began erupting. Super-heated rocks, glowing red, spewed forth and rained down on us. From within the crater, a growing ash cloud billowed into the sky, swallowing the sun, engulfing us in seconds. We ran, panicked, scrambling to keep on our feet, dodging burning chunks of rock as large as small cars. We were pummeled by fiery projectiles of all sizes, inflicting burns and injuries. We tried wildly to outrun the rocks and ash, praying all the while for God's deliverance.

Finally, miraculously, most of us were able to reunite near the trailhead where we would begin to head down the mountain. Together we limped through the eerie twilight of the still billowing ash cloud, keenly aware that our lives had been spared only by God's grace. Once we reached the tree line, we improvised a hillside emergency room, collected water from the mountain stream, and built crude splints and stretchers for the seriously wounded. We estimated that with the various injuries slowing our pace, the remaining descent would take close to nine hours.

The rain was unrelenting as our group trudged down slippery Mount Merapi. Most of the way I followed behind my friend John, gripping his jeans by the back belt loop in an attempt to keep him from having to put his full weight on his broken leg. We forged a small stream at one point and sang together to calm the stress and anxiety, doing our best to keep the more traumatized in our group from slipping into shock. As we worked to meet each other's needs in those hours of desperation, our spontaneous community was drawn closely together. Early on, we were a group rejoicing in our cultural diversity and in the grand adventure that lay ahead, now we worked together to survive. We suffered, served, and mourned together. For a couple of those injured on the mountain, the help that community offered meant the difference between survival or perishing, stranded and alone.

Sadly, though God has designed us to rely on each other, we often value community only in emergencies such as I experienced on Mount Merapi. We can overlook the needs of those around us and our own need for others as we labor in isolation to live our lives. The truth is we are by and large a people who idolize independence and self-reliance. From Clint Eastwood to Ironman, our cultural heroes are rugged individualists. They don't need anyone's assistance, gifting, or provision to get them out of any predicament. It's no surprise then that the body of Christ in our country is so challenged in experiencing community in the way God intends.

THE ANTIDOTE TO INDIVIDUALISM

As I searched the Scriptures to discover God's "essentials" for community as He has designed it, the first one I encountered was the antithesis of our rugged American individualism. In fact, as I spend time with Christ followers in other parts of the world, it is clear that they tend to understand and embody it more naturally than those in the United States.

Community as God intended is meant to be interdependent. We are not created to go it alone or face the struggles of life on our own. Because our independent nature runs so deeply, this is a difficult truth for us to embrace. As believers, our influence in the world is not based on our abilities, but it grows out of our interconnectedness with God and with others. In fact, God's influence in our lives and our kingdom influence in the world are dependent on us living out this value.

Elton Trueblood puts it this way:

Jesus did not leave a book. He did not leave an army. He did not leave an organization, in the ordinary sense. What He left, instead, was a little redemptive fellowship made up of extremely common people whose total impact was miraculous. Though the members were individually unworthy, the fellowship which they came to share was so far superior to the sum of its parts that it was not only able to survive and endure, but finally to dominate and to save.[1]

Previously I wrote about the powerful impact of a small, humble hobbit in the LORD OF THE RINGS trilogy. Despite how powerfully God can use an individual who is humble and dependent on Him, He has not designed us to do it alone. In the Tolkien novel-made-movie *The Fellowship of the Rings*, the example of an interdependent community could not be more vivid. At the Council of Elrond, a diverse band of comrades come together to set out on the great task of taking the ring of power to be destroyed in Mordor. Together, they make an interesting group, each one with his own flaws but together a formidable force. That group is composed of four hobbits: Frodo Baggins, Sam, Pippin, and Merry; two men: Strider and Boromir; the elf prince Legolas; Gimli the dwarf; and Gandalf the wizard. After watching the trilogy one could easily list the varied strengths and weaknesses of each of the members of the fellowship. As the adventure progresses, each has the opportunity to make a unique contribution through the use of his gifts and strengths. So life in God's kingdom is meant to reflect this same interdependence. As Trueblood describes, our "total impact" will be "miraculous."

THE INTERDEPENDENT NATURE OF GOD

Relational interdependence is an important characteristic of kingdom community. Because man is made in the image of God, you would expect to see community in the nature of God. Gilbert Bilezikian writes, "Whatever community exists as a result of God's creation, it is only a reflection of an eternal reality that is intrinsic to the being of God. Because God is eternally one, when he created in his image, he created oneness."[2]

The early church fathers, like John Damascene, used the term *perichoresis* to describe the mutual interworking and dynamic interdependence of the Godhead. Basically, *perichoresis* describes the idea that the Father, Son, and Spirit are united and exist only in relation to one another. Clearly, God provides for us the ultimate example of interdependence and unity.

As difficult as it is for our human minds to grasp, while there is only one God, He exists as an interdependent Trinity. And Scripture portrays our one triune God as an intensely personal, loving, and interacting community consisting of the Father, Son, and Holy Spirit. We get glimpses of this interactive community working together:

- During creation, as Father, Son, and Holy Spirit worked to make the universe. In Genesis 1:26, God says, "Let *us* make man in *our* image, in our likeness" (emphasis added). The use of *us* and *our* was almost unanimously interpreted by the early church fathers, such as Augustine, as a reference to the Trinity.[3] The Scriptures portray the involvement of all the members: Spirit (see Genesis 1:2; Job 26:13), Son (see John 1:3; Colossians 1:16-17), and Father (see Jeremiah 10:12; Hebrews 11:3).
- At Jesus' Baptism. In Matthew's account of Jesus' baptism, there is another glimpse of the community of God collaborating at a pivotal point in human history. He writes, "At that moment heaven was opened, and he saw the Spirit

of God descending like a dove and lighting on him. And a voice from heaven said, 'This is my Son, whom I love; with him I am well pleased'" (3:16-17). Those onlookers who were privileged to see the beginning of the ministry of Christ had a unique opportunity to see the three persons of the Trinity in action, each doing a part to usher in a revolutionary season of God's history! The Son, Jesus, was the one at the center of the stage. The supporting actor, the Holy Spirit, came out of the heavens, and the booming voice of the Father narrated, announced, and affirmed the ministry of Jesus. Remarkably, the same is true in each of our spiritual lives. The Father has drawn us by His love and spoken to us through His Word. The Son has bought us through His blood, shed on the cross. And the Holy Spirit now dwells in us and is working to transform us to reflect the Son.

• In the giving of the Holy Spirit. Jesus had made it clear to His disciples that the Father had promised and would be sending the Holy Spirit (see John 14:16,26; Luke 24:49). Through the empowering of the Holy Spirit, the Father, Son, and Holy Spirit worked together to give birth to the early church.

Thus we see three collaborative activities of God that demonstrate the kind of community He desires for His followers. Because we are made in the image of God, you would expect the interdependence we see in God to be reflected in our spiritual community. In the last chapter we saw four models of God-designed community: Adam and Eve, the nation of Israel, the disciples of Jesus, and the church. In each case we see that community as God designed is relational and purposeful. From these examples of the interdependent nature of God, we see that the community of the Trinity is also relational and purposeful. Jesus' prayer in John 17 points to this interdependent unity as God's desire for His people:

My prayer is not for them alone. I pray also for those who will believe in me through their message, that all of them may be one, Father, just as you are in me and I am in you. May they also be in us so that the world may believe that you have sent me. . . . I in them and you in me. May they be brought to complete unity to let the world know that you sent me and have loved them even as you have loved me. (verses 20-21,23)

As God's people, made in His image, it makes sense that we would live in community for this noteworthy reason: God Himself lives in community. Our great God, the triune three in one, is Father, Son, and Holy Spirit. God has made and designed us to experience the same kind of interdependence with one another.

THREE FOUNDATIONS FOR INTERDEPENDENT COMMUNITY

What does it actually look like to live like this? The Bible gives us three identifiers for interdependence that reflect the heart of Christ.

Loving Service

Jesus' whole view of humanity and relationships emphasizes interdependence. His call to love (see John 13:34) and to serve (see Mark 10:43-45) builds a foundation for biblical interdependence. If a person has two shirts or extra food, he or she is to share with those in need (see Luke 3:11). The law of relationships is summed up in treating others as you would have them treat you (see Matthew 7:12; Luke 6:31). While the religious leaders of Jesus' day defined spirituality in religious terms and religious observances, Jesus clearly defined spirituality as how we relate with God and with one another. Our spiritual life is best assessed not by our observing a set of guidelines or showing up for religious meetings but by how we love God and one another (see Matthew 22:34-40).

Fellowship

The biblical word *koinonia* is a concept that flows straight out of the love and service that Jesus desires to see in our interdependent relationships. It is commonly translated in the New Testament as "fellowship." Jesus' closest disciple, John, wrote: "We proclaim to you what we have seen and heard, so that you also may have fellowship with us. And our fellowship is with the Father and with his Son, Jesus Christ" (1 John 1:3).

Fellowship means joint ownership or partnership. The word is not a soft or sentimental idea, but describes deeply mutual relationships. The potential reality of this kind of intertwined relationship is first seen, as John says, in our relationship with the Father and with the Son. Bonhoeffer states it strongly:

> *Christianity means community through Jesus Christ and in Jesus Christ. No Christian community is more or less than this. Whether it be a brief, single encounter or the daily fellowship of years, Christian community is only this. We belong to one another only through and in Jesus Christ.*[4]

As we have said before, the life of a Christ follower finds its roots and power in our relationship with God. This is true of our interdependence in community; it is rooted in our fellowship with God.

The same kind of mutual fellowship is present in the relationships seen in the early church:

> *All the believers were together and had everything in common. Selling their possessions and goods, they gave to anyone as he had need. Every day they continued to meet together in the temple courts. They broke bread in their homes and ate together with glad and sincere hearts, praising God and enjoying the favor of all the people. And the Lord added to their number daily those who were being saved.* (Acts 2:44-47)

These believers were devoted to fellowship (see Acts 2:42). Have you ever experienced friendships that "were together and had everything in common"? The interdependence of that early group of Jesus' followers was seen vividly in their sharing of possessions, giving to the ones who had needs, sharing meals, and worshipping God together.

The "One Anothers"

The phrase "one another" occurs more than thirty times in the New Testament letters. The biblical letters were written to communities of Christ followers who, like us, desperately needed guidance in how to relate in ways that honor God.

The words associated with how we are to interact with one another are challenging and invasive. These are not words that allow us to stay in our houses with windows and doors shut, watching the Lifestyle Network or *SportsCenter*! We are called to forgive, accept, bear burdens, encourage, love, confess sins, honor, submit, and spur on one another, to name a few. If we would measure our relationships by these words on a regular basis and act on them, our lives would be healthier and the watching world would knock down doors to join us! Consider these examples:

> *Be completely humble and gentle; be patient, bearing with* one another *in love. . . . Be kind and compassionate to one another, forgiving each other, just as in Christ God forgave you.* (Ephesians 4:2,32, emphasis added)

> *Bear with each other and forgive whatever grievances you may have against* one another. *Forgive as the Lord forgave you.* (Colossians 3:13, emphasis added)

> *And let us consider how we may spur* one another *on toward love and good deeds. Let us not give up meeting together, as*

some are in the habit of doing, but let us encourage one another. (Hebrews 10:24-25, emphasis added)

Brothers, do not slander one another. (James 4:11, emphasis added)

Finally, all of you, live in harmony with one another; *be sympathetic, love as brothers, be compassionate and humble.* (1 Peter 3:8, emphasis added)

We were not designed to win battles singlehandedly, despite what Matt Damon, Bruce Willis, and Angelina Jolie seem to be able to pull off! Interdependent Jesus-centered community is established and deepened when we choose to live life fully and faithfully with a few close friends.

Several years ago, we were part of a group of couples who had made a covenant together to live in community in the ways that God encourages in the Scriptures. During one particularly difficult season, two of the couples in that group were experiencing challenges in life, family, and their jobs. One couple that had just started a business was severely challenged financially. Another couple that had just gone through a very difficult pregnancy also had an unforeseen medical crisis. As I look back on that season, I wish that we would have done more to help. But, in the midst of our own lives and challenges, each of the other couples worked to lend a hand and contribute to the needs of those two couples as they navigated rough waters. The interdependence that God commands us to enter into is demanding—it calls us to live sacrificially and to reflect the spirit of Jesus, whose love caused Him to give up His life.

LEANING QUESTIONS

Our culture battles against us as we strive to live interdependently.

The typical pace of American life doesn't lend itself toward deeply connected relationships. And with our high-performance culture, how can any of us lean on others and allow others to lean on us? For some of us, it is an unwillingness to trust others with our lives. And some of us have been burned and hurt deeply when we trusted others.

Pam and I regularly assess our lives and ask ourselves the questions, *Who are we leaning on?* and *Who are we allowing to lean on us?* We always want to have a small group of friends where there is "mutual leaning." In many of our lives we can think of people we depend on and people who depend on us. We have found that our most healthy seasons of life were characterized by a few close relationships of interdependence.

There is no reason to wait for some unforeseen disaster to thrust you into interdependent relationships. The only way forward against the culture that tends to isolate us is to initiate with a few people to learn and grow into relationships that reflect biblical interdependence. Because we are designed for these kinds of relationships, God's influence in our lives and our kingdom influence in the world is dependent on our living out this value.

John Eldredge put it this way in his book *Waking the Dead*:

> God is calling together little communities of the heart, to fight for one another and for the hearts of those who have not yet been set free. That camaraderie, that intimacy, that incredible impact by a few stouthearted souls — that is available. It is the Christian life as Jesus gave it to us. It is completely normal.[5]

As we think about interdependence and the kind of community we know we need, most of us realize that there are not many people who are *current* with our lives and have access to our hearts and struggles. We've heard of the statistics that speak of a crisis of loneliness and isolation in our world today. What would it feel like to *know* and to really be *known* in a way that fosters the community that God intends? We'll tackle this next.

QUESTIONS FOR REFLECTION

- Who are you leaning on these days? Who is leaning on you?
- Think of two or three people with whom you could grow in interdependence. In the lives of these people, what ways could you intentionally love or serve them; mutually depend on each other; forgive them, bear their burdens, or encourage them?

CHAPTER 11

AUTHENTIC VULNERABILITY

Without confession we are a community hiding from the truth.

— JOHN ORTBERG

THE RECENT PROLIFERATION of social media, such as Facebook and a myriad other means for connectivity, makes research published in 2006 by the *American Sociological Review* both surprising and disturbing. The study of social isolation in America showed a sharp decrease in the number of confidants that individuals list as members of a core group with whom they feel free to discuss personal or important matters. In 2004, the average American had just two close friends, down from three in 1985. Those reporting no confidants jumped from 10 percent in 1985 to 25 percent in 2004. Increasingly, individuals report no close friends beyond household members.[1]

I talked with a twentysomething friend who wondered whether the ease and speed of social-media interactions may have an effect that actually negates true community building. Some people we meet in my travels with The Navigators have hundreds of "friends" on Facebook but admit that they wonder if they have anyone to talk to in a crisis. It's possible that Internet-based community leaves many in trouble if the only intimate relationships cultivated are with ones who remain safely uncommitted or unable to enter into our lives fully. If or when something goes awry in those relationships, a simple "defriending" severs the ties. A password change or deleted e-mail address means never having to say you're sorry or even good-bye. Many young adults are becoming aware of this dynamic and are changing their expectations of social media and how they use it. More often than ever before, many in our culture are living lives of isolation with no one to confide in and no safe relationship for sharing personal struggles.

The second characteristic of God-designed community is authentic vulnerability—distinguished by genuine openness, confession, and dependence on others for help. Each of us needs people around who offer us a safe opportunity to be fully human and completely open about how we are really doing. We need friends who will not be shocked by the depth of our sin and missteps. We need people who will receive us with grace when we mess up, walk with us through struggles, and guide us to healing or restoration.

The word *vulnerability* has a number of definitions and can be a confusing concept. The founders of Leadership Catalyst have made a helpful distinction between transparency and vulnerability: "Transparency has value but is limited. Vulnerability is my choice to let you know me, to have access to my life, to teach and influence me—to not only see the cracks, but to fill them."[2]

I am indebted to the teachers at Leadership Catalyst for their help as I have come to embrace some of these ideas. Let me interpret a bit what is meant here:

1. Many people are transparent. Transparency is a willingness to reveal ourselves to others as we really are. Transparency is important and good, but it is not always enough.
2. Vulnerability, as I am using it in this chapter, is not only revealing who I am but also allowing one or two other trusted friends to influence and direct me in my areas of weakness.
3. We all have "cracks," inadequacies and weaknesses, in our

lives. In vulnerability, we choose to not only allow people to see them, but also allow them to address them and help us to fill those "cracks" or weaknesses.

The dictionary definition of *vulnerable* means to be susceptible to wounds or harm. The Bible says, "Faithful are the wounds of a friend; profuse are the kisses of an enemy" (Proverbs 27:6, ESV). The health of our relationships in Christ and the strength of our community together depends on the permission we give to one another to speak honestly (even to the point of wounding) about the real and deeply personal issues of life. We do well to make ourselves susceptible and vulnerable to a few close friends.

In his book *Life Together*, Dietrich Bonhoeffer speaks of the importance of a community that welcomes the less-than-perfect among us:

He who is alone with his sin is utterly alone. It may be that Christians notwithstanding corporate worship, common prayer, and all their fellowship and service, may still be left to their loneliness. The final break-through to fellowship does not occur, because, though they have fellowship with one another as believers and as devout people, they do not have fellowship as the undevout, as sinners. The pious fellowship permits no one to be a sinner. So everybody must conceal his sin from himself and from the fellowship. We dare not be sinners. Many Christians are unthinkably horrified when a real sinner is suddenly discovered among the righteous. So we remain alone with our sin, living in lies and hypocrisy. The fact is we are sinners.[3]

I remember one time in particular when participating in this sort of authentic and open community helped me to stop and critically consider my behavior well before damage occurred. I'm changing most particulars here, but feel the story will illustrate our theme.

In one particular ministry setting, I worked closely with a woman who was going through some personal struggles. In the course of our work together, I found myself relating with her at a level of the heart that began to set off some caution lights for me. I knew that allowing my heart to engage in this relational situation was not healthy. I was uncomfortable with it and grew increasingly uneasy.

One day I was walking and sharing with a good friend, Tony. Now Tony and I didn't have any kind of formal relationship of accountability, but he noticed I seemed troubled and invited me to talk more over coffee. When we got together, I asked him for his opinion regarding what I was struggling with. It was the first time I had shared this kind of struggle so openly with someone. I was frightened of what Tony might think and almost didn't say anything to him. I'm so thankful I took the risk and told him what was going on.

He didn't flinch, but listened to my heart and entered into my situation. Very quickly things changed for me. I had someone "in my corner" with me. I had a new sense of confidence. Because of his commitment to me, I was no longer afraid that I would go in a direction that wasn't healthy and was able to take the steps I needed to provide boundaries. With my more open relationship with Tony, I had a new ally to walk with me in future challenges. (I say new, because my wife, Pam, has and continues to be this kind of ally in various life issues.) Tony and Pam represent protectors for me in those areas of my life where, on my own, I may not get it right.

FOUR STEPS FOR DEVELOPING AUTHENTIC COMMUNITY

Vulnerability, like interdependence, can seem difficult to attain. How can we move into relationships where this is accepted and even expected? Four Scripture passages act as guides toward developing relationships that offer authentic vulnerability.

Bear with and Forgive

Bear with each other and forgive whatever grievances you may have against one another. Forgive as the Lord forgave you. (Colossians 3:13)

In verse 12, Paul describes a culture of grace by listing traits that should characterize God's chosen people. The final trait is patience. Verse 13 could easily be seen as an elaboration on the characteristic of patience. Two ideas undergird the culture that will provide a safe place for people to be vulnerable. The first idea is that of "bearing with" — putting up with the unpleasant traits or weaknesses that might irritate. The second idea, forgiveness, is grounded in the model of how Jesus forgives — lavishly. Clearly, when friends make a practice of bearing with and forgiving, a foundation is laid for authenticity and openness despite weaknesses and struggles.

Confess to One Another

Therefore confess your sins to each other and pray for each other so that you may be healed. (James 5:16)

While in some traditions followers of Christ confess their sins to a spiritual leader, this verse makes it clear that confession is a key competency for everyone in community. True community is characterized by relationships in which confession is natural. We need kingdom friends who know us, our weaknesses, and our sins. And the command to confess gives us the responsibility to be ready to hear of our brothers' and sisters' sin.

Submit to One Another

Submit to one another out of reverence for Christ. (Ephesians 5:21)

We are to yield and surrender ourselves to the influence and direction of other believers. In other Scripture passages we are told to submit to governing authorities, to spiritual leaders, and to God, but this verse has a much broader application. In the body of Christ, submission, a yielding and surrendering to one another, is to characterize all our relationships. I am not talking here of inappropriate submission to authoritative tyrants, but healthy, daily submitting who we are to a few others. Submission is the act that makes vulnerability not just a willingness to admit weakness or sin, but also the act of giving a few friends permission to address and speak directly to those sins and weaknesses, providing accountability for us in those areas. Notice also that our submission is grounded in our reverence for Christ. It's natural because it's built on the same attitude with which we approach the Lord.

Share the Painful Load

Carry each other's burdens, and in this way you will fulfill the law of Christ. (Galatians 6:2)

Authentic vulnerability only works if we in the body are ready to share the load of life with those around us. Are we willing to lend our shoulders to the emotional, spiritual, and physical burdens our friends are experiencing? Tony did that for me when he provided a safe place to confess my temptation to sin. Earlier in his letter to the Galatians, the apostle Paul said that the entire law is summed up in the command to "love your neighbor as yourself" (Galatians 5:14). Clearly Paul puts the bearing of one another's burdens high on the list as a reflection of love. In the particular context Paul is addressing, what he means by shouldering burdens is clear. It has to do with a gentle response to those who have fallen to temptation (see Galatians 6:1,3). It is not enough for people to be willing to confess sin and submit themselves to other Christ followers. The community of Christ must be willing to shoulder the burdens of those who continue to struggle with some area of sin.

CREATING A SAFE PLACE

When one of our children was about ten years old, I began to notice that this child seemed hesitant to talk with me about weaknesses and struggles. At bedtime, I would go in, sing a couple of bedtime songs, and pray. In the course of the time I would ask how things were going. The answer was almost always the same: "Fine." Ten minutes later, Pam would go into that child's bedroom and follow a similar pattern of conversation but often with dramatically different results. If our child were struggling with something at school, the story would tumble forth, sometimes with tears. I felt horrible. Why would our child confide in Pam but not in me?

I soon discovered, through the help of a mentor, that I was not creating a safe place for our child to be vulnerable and authentic. In fact, I had created an environment where this child was downright afraid to be honest. I had created a culture in that relationship that was characterized by judgment, a lack of forbearance, and a lack of safety. It took years to change the relationship I had with that child, and I'm still working on it. In our family relationships and friendships with other believers we will only experience the depth of fellowship God desires when we move forward in authentic vulnerability.

John Ortberg, teaching pastor at Menlo Park Presbyterian Church, speaks of the importance of authenticity in the context of community:

> *We all wear masks. We hide from each other. It's part of our fallenness. . . . Confession is the appropriate disclosure of my*

brokenness, temptations, sin, and victories for the purpose of
healing, forgiveness, and spiritual growth. Without confession
we are a community hiding from the truth. I know what it's
like to do church with people who wear masks. I've attended
very nice churches where people smiled, talked about their jobs
or the weather, but never really removed their masks and
revealed themselves.[4]

As I've described in previous chapters, when Pam and I were facing months of turmoil and eventual termination in a church where we served on staff, we struggled with balancing a desire to not gossip and honor Christ in the situation with a need to maintain our own spiritual health and sanity. Our lifeline came through a few carefully chosen confidants in the form of a small covenant group. That group proved to be a safe haven where we could air our frustrations, share our emotional struggles, and be fully who we were at the time, as ugly as that could be! The friends in that group walked with us, loved us, prayed for us, and allowed us an opportunity to be real in our pain, sin, and vulnerability. They also challenged us and helped us see our own sin and missteps. Though I was fired from that job, Pam and I survived and grew through that painful experience. Our survival and growth was due to God's grace made manifest in that dear community of friends. We are still connected with them today, despite the miles and years.

Making waves for the kingdom of God is not meant to be a solo experience. Our influence for Christ over the long haul demands that we not go it alone and that we have a small group of people around us we can lean on and who will walk with us during our darkest hours. Recently I missed an opportunity to love and walk with a good friend who was going through a tough time. When I asked him why he hadn't told me about his troubles, he confided that he thought I was too busy. Many believers find themselves too busy for the kind of friendships I've described, or we get spread thin, trying to sustain deep relationships with too many people.

An onlooking world desperately needs to see the difference that Christ makes in our relationships. They long to have the freedom to be themselves and to experience the gracious safety true community in Jesus offers. The more we experience it, the more they will see it and desire it. Moreover, without the influence of a community of committed friends we ourselves may not experience the change that God desires. It is that topic we will consider next: the powerful transforming influence of community.

QUESTIONS FOR REFLECTION

- Do you have one or two people in your life you can be transparent with, but with whom you can also be vulnerable? Who are they? If not, who could you move toward relationally to develop that kind of friendship?
- Are you a "safe place" for other people to be themselves? Are other people able to come to you with their areas of weakness or sin? Are there ways you could grow as a safer person? What ways would you consider? Pray for God's help.

CHAPTER 12

TRANSFORMING RELATIONSHIPS

Jonathan became one in spirit with David, and he loved him us himself.

— SAMUEL (1 SAMUEL 18:1)

THE YEAR AFTER I graduated from college, I spent a year with a group of six other young men in a mentoring and ministry program that later became Doulos Ministries. We lived, worked, and fought together. We spent much time with ministry founder Richard Beach, who continued to be my dear friend and mentor until his death to cancer in 2010. Under Richard's leadership during that idyllic year, our raucous household of young bucks spent much time gnawing on Scripture and striving to meaningfully serve young people in and around Branson, Missouri.

There are many stories I could tell about the year and the character development you can imagine occurring when a group of immature and headstrong young men make a commitment to live and work and study together. We began as a ragtag group and ended the year still a good part ragtag, but with an important difference: God's power had a grip on each of us and was working mightily through our influence on each other as we made ourselves vulnerable and learned to lean on one another.

One of our assignments during the year was to select one of the fruit of the Spirit described in Galatians 5:22-23 and prepare a teaching session on that topic. We all put a lot of time into our study and preparation. Most of us put together well-planned, well-studied, biblical lessons on our chosen topic. We were all encouraged and challenged by what we heard of peace, gentleness, kindness, patience, self-control, and faithfulness. However, only one of the lessons stands out to me still.

My friend Kris "Coop" Cooper had as his assignment, love, the first fruit in that familiar list. Coop started by speaking very briefly about various passages having to do with love. Then he began describing the month leading up to his presentation. Coop said he had observed each of us closely. He'd painstakingly noted the things we liked. He noticed the foods we snarfed, the soft drinks we chugged. He even noticed the things he owned that we admired. Then, after reading us several Scriptures about love as God defines it, Coop pulled out six paper bags. Each was labeled with one of our names and each of those bags was filled to overflowing with specific items that the designated recipient enjoyed.

Coop handed me a bag filled with candy and a liter of Coke. That pleased me, but what shocked me was the next item I found when I reached into the bag. I pulled out Coop's favorite high school baseball jersey. He had worn it many days during the year, and I had mentioned to him how much I loved that jersey. Serving, giving, and loving were not among my strengths as a young man. The idea that my buddy Coop would give up something as special to him as that baseball jersey did not make any sense to me until he went on to discuss 1 John 4:9-10: "This is how God showed his love among us: He sent his one and only Son into the world that we might live through him. This is love: not that we loved God, but that he loved us and sent his Son as an atoning sacrifice for our sins."

He emphasized that God's love is seen most clearly in His willingness to serve us and give sacrificially to us through His Son Jesus. For Coop, the time he spent watching and planning to love us each uniquely and then his presentation of the gifts to each of us was his best attempt to emulate God's sacrificial love. His example was quite effective. It helped plant in me a deep desire to live and love in that same way. Coop's obedience yielded a lifelong impression and strong example in my life, a memorable object lesson proving the words of Proverbs 27:17, "As iron sharpens iron, so a friend sharpens a friend" (NLTSE).

In fact after thirty years I still remember and am being transformed by many lessons embodied in that community of men filled by the Spirit of God. You see, transformation is not designed to happen primarily through the contagious enthusiasm of spiritual superstars, but through the lives of everyday people living in the context of community. We'll look more deeply at the topic of transformation in part 4, but in this chapter we will explore how God uses the influence of other Christ followers to mold us more into His character.

GOD'S INSTRUMENTS OF CHANGE

King David was a changed man because of the community of influencers God provided for him. The life story of this Old Testament "Braveheart" is a riveting and dramatic example of the transforming power of God working in one imperfect man's life through a circle of imperfect people.

As a young man, David is alternately a hero, a liar, and a fraud (he feigned insanity to get what he wanted). He is self-dependent, self-indulgent, and an adulterer. And then, sometimes in the midst of his stinkiest behavior, he gave glory to God. He was intermittently fiercely respectful of God's anointed one, Saul, and repeatedly repentant of his own sins. David was a lifelong learner, a work in progress, and one famously described as "a man after God's own heart."

This man was a human study in contrasts, to put it mildly. Consider the words he penned at the end of his life:

The Spirit of the Lord *spoke through me;*
    his word was on my tongue.
The God of Israel spoke,
    the Rock of Israel said to me:
"When one rules over men in righteousness,
    when he rules in the fear of God,
he is like the light of morning at sunrise
    on a cloudless morning,
like the brightness after rain
    that brings the grass from the earth."
Is not my house right with God?
    Has he not made with me an everlasting covenant,
    arranged and secured in every part?
Will he not bring to fruition my salvation
    and grant me my every desire? (2 Samuel 23:2-5)

Certainly one of David's admirable qualities was the flexibility he maintained even into old age. While some people grow hard and stubborn as the years go by, David's attitude actually improved. His increasing tendency toward pleasing and seeking God and the steadily more faithful and meek character that emerged through that pursuit, is obvious in his final words, as he rests in God's promises and eternal character.

The life of David is an encouragement to all of us who are not changed in a moment, but over a lifetime. While he wobbled back and forth, never ceasing to be an imperfect man, the shaping hand of God continued to mold him over the course of his life. While his early years of leadership were about all things David—his survival, his satisfaction, and his ego—David's enduring testimony is that of a God-fearing man who brought blessing to those entrusted to him.

But how did this notable change of heart and habit occur? David, more than any other leader we see in the Old Testament, was willing to allow others to speak into his life, acting as God's instruments of change.

Four people had particular influence in David's life.

Early in David's adult life he is pursued and attacked by none other than Saul, the king of Israel. David had already received the memo that he was anointed by God to be the next king of Israel, but at the time Saul was still on the throne. Scripture says that Saul was affected by a contrary spirit. The crazy king was compulsively jealous of David and was trying to kill him.

It is then, in the nick of time, that Saul's son Jonathan entered the story. Jonathan was the first of David's four community mentors, although he had every reason to side with his father. Until David's anointing, Jonathan was the heir apparent to the throne. Jonathan could have easily justified maintaining allegiance to his father either on a political basis or simply on the basis of self-preservation. Yet when the heat came on and it became obvious that Saul was out to kill David, Jonathan became instead a trusted friend. The Bible describes their friendship:

> After David had finished talking with Saul, Jonathan became one in spirit with David, and he loved him as himself. . . . And Jonathan made a covenant with David because he loved him as himself. Jonathan took off the robe he was wearing and gave it to David, along with his tunic, and even his sword, his bow and his belt. (1 Samuel 18:1,3-4)

Jonathan bestowed on David the symbols of his own status as prince—his robe, his tunic, his sword, his bow, and his belt. These gifts reflected Jonathan's commitment to David's future as Israel's king. Jonathan also saved David's life and served as an advocate for him before his father, Saul:

Saul told his son Jonathan and all the attendants to kill David. But Jonathan was very fond of David and warned him, "My father Saul is looking for a chance to kill you. Be on your guard tomorrow morning; go into hiding and stay there. . . ." Jonathan spoke well of David to Saul his father and said to him, "Let not the king do wrong to his servant David; he has not wronged you, and what he has done has benefited you greatly. He took his life in his hands when he killed the Philistine." (1 Samuel 19:1-2,4-5)

In 1 Samuel 20, Jonathan continued to watch out for David and protect him from Saul. A few chapters later, while David was still running from Saul, he and his men had a run-in with a selfish and mean-spirited landowner named Nabal. David's men had been protecting Nabal's herds, but when they asked Nabal for some help he responded by cursing them. David and his men responded in a typically macho, Old-Testament manner. They mounted their steeds and set out to kill Nabal and all his men. It is on that journey that David met Abigail, Nabal's wife, described as an intelligent and beautiful woman. She is the second strong influencer of David we'll consider.

When Abigail heard what had transpired and what David and his men had planned for her husband, she sprang into action. She managed to head off David at the pass, before he had a chance to murderously vent his anger at Nabal. Abigail approached David on the road. Her donkeys were loaded with gifts for him and his men. She presented bread, wine, sheep, and cakes. She diffused David's rage and atoned her husband's nasty outburst with these wise words:

Now since the LORD has kept you, my master, from bloodshed and from avenging yourself with your own hands, as surely as the LORD lives and as you live, may your enemies and all who intend to harm my master be like Nabal. And let this gift,

which your servant has brought to my master, be given to the
men who follow you. Please forgive your servant's offense, for
the LORD will certainly make a lasting dynasty for my master,
because he fights the LORD's battles. Let no wrongdoing be
found in you as long as you live. (1 Samuel 25:26-28)

David allowed Abigail's words to influence him. He stopped in his
tracks and came to his senses. This bold woman's wisdom kept the
future king from foolish bloodshed and protected her own errant husband. Abigail honored David and blessed him. In the process, no
doubt, David's character was influenced. Later, after Abigail's husband
died, David took her to be his wife.

The prophet Nathan is the third example of a person who had a
dramatic influence on David's character development. The story is a
familiar one. After David had been king of Israel for some time, he
committed adultery with Bathsheba. When she became pregnant,
David tried to hide his sin with a complicated deception that resulted
in the death of Bathsheba's husband, Uriah. At tremendous personal
risk, Nathan, a prophet and part of David's circle of community, confronted David (see 2 Samuel 12:1-9). Nathan had the courage to do
the right thing, seeking to bring David to repentance and restoration.
Nathan also brought a word from the Lord regarding God's judgment
on David and his household (see 2 Samuel 12:10-12).

The Scripture says that it was the Lord who sent Nathan to David.
Likewise, He is the one who calls us to enter into one another's lives
and help to bring about repentance and restoration. We have a
common responsibility to participate in community in order to see the
Lord's transformation. It's important to notice David's response and
God's forgiveness: "Then David said to Nathan, 'I have sinned against
the LORD.' Nathan replied, 'The LORD has taken away your sin.
You are not going to die'" (2 Samuel 12:13).

Though David's household and future were deeply impacted by
the consequences of his sin, David also was affected by God's grace,

mercy, and forgiveness. Nathan was an important instrument God used to set David back on the right path.

Israeli army leader Joab is the fourth influencer of David. This man was one of David's nephews, his sister's son, and the brother of Abishai and Asahel. David had known Joab and his brothers since they were all young men, and they were numbered among David's mighty men (see 1 Chronicles 11). Joab was far from a perfect leader, but his commitment to David was very strong. At a key juncture in David's life, Joab brought him a word of counsel that helped to preserve David's honor and authority.

Absalom, David's son, had rebelled and pulled off a coup. David and those loyal to him were driven out of Jerusalem. Later when a battle ensued, David's men killed Absalom, preserving David's throne. However, despite the good news that the rebellion was over, David wept uncontrollably at his son's death. The word spread through the army, those who had just put their lives on the line to quell Absalom's takeover, that David was so deeply grieved. Joab, David's friend and loyal commander came to David to help him see his error:

> *Today you have humiliated all your men, who have just saved your life and the lives of your sons and daughters and the lives of your wives and concubines. You love those who hate you and hate those who love you. You have made it clear today that the commanders and their men mean nothing to you. I see that you would be pleased if Absalom were alive today and all of us were dead. Now go out and encourage your men. I swear by the LORD that if you don't go out, not a man will be left with you by nightfall. This will be worse for you than all the calamities that have come upon you from your youth till now.* (2 Samuel 19:5-7)

While Joab's actions were not always noble, he was part of David's community and a trusted friend. His words penetrated

David's heart and grief and gave him courage to respond rightly: "So the king got up and took his seat in the gateway. When the men were told, 'The king is sitting in the gateway,' they all came before him" (2 Samuel 19:8).

Because of Joab's exhortation, David was able to move forward and come before his men who had put their lives in harm's way for him.

There are others who walked alongside David and influenced him like Samuel, Gad, Abiathar, Ittai the Gittite, and Hushai the Arkite. Just as God used people as His instruments in David's life, it is His design for us to be part of a community that has a transforming influence in our lives.

Do you have a community like that around *yourself*?

John Ortberg speaks of the role community is to have in our lives,

> *Years ago, while on vacation, I was going to fix something on the grill. I made a pile of charcoal, I poured a few gallons of lighter fluid over them, and I started the fire. My son was just fascinated by fire, as most young boys are. He asked what I was doing, and I told him. "There's something about the way these little briquettes are constructed that when you put them together, the fire glows and they get real hot. And if you isolate one it cools off quickly. It loses the fire. But when they stick together, there's fire, because they feed off each other. God designed them to work that way. . . ." Personalities united — people in community — contain more of God and his transforming power than isolated individuals. We should not be surprised that transformation requires community; it's how God designed us.[1]*

The enemy of our soul loves to keep us apart, where we grow cool and ineffective. Instead, we must recognize that one of the most precious gifts God gives in this life is people. It is through their influence, words, and actions that we are changed. We do not grow more like Jesus without each other. Despite the strong messages of our do-it-yourself world, one sure-fire way to send generational waves of kingdom impact through eternity is to be part of a community of friends committed to experiencing life together in authentic discipleship to Jesus Christ.

QUESTIONS FOR REFLECTION

- Name one or two people who, because of their friendship, have helped to lead you to be more like Jesus? Thank God for those friendships.
- Is there an older person who could be a Samuel to you, speaking into your life and mentoring you? What could you do to initiate relationship with that person and ask for his or her help?
- Are there peers, people in the same season of life, who you could intentionally move toward in order to develop a relationship that is mutually transforming? Who are they? What could be your next step in those relationships?

CHAPTER 13

AN ETERNAL PURPOSE

May they be brought to complete unity to let the world know that
you sent me and have loved them even as you have loved me.

— JESUS (JOHN 17:23)

AS I WRITE, a human drama is unfolding in Japan. On Friday, March 11, 2011, a magnitude nine earthquake and a powerful tsunami devastated the island nation. The ongoing crisis centers on the Fukushima nuclear plant, where the tsunami has crippled and damaged the plant's cooling systems, making it susceptible to meltdown. Radiation is leaking, residents of other countries are being evacuated, and the world looks on and prays.

On the world stage of this drama, a community of heroes is risking their lives to battle the malicious nuclear forces at that stricken plant. Known as the Fukushima 50, they are workers who have remained behind to assess the damage and cool the handicapped reactors with seawater to avert a potential radiation catastrophe that would put innumerable human lives at risk. Several days after the event their numbers grew to over 120, including experts and workers from other plants.

These workers, standing against disaster together, represent a community of unimaginable courage and humbling heroism, bent on saving others. I sat watching a news report with my eyes brimming, and I considered the risk these few were taking for the many. One woman told of her husband, one of the remaining workers, who after forty years was due to retire in September.

Communities of Jesus followers also have a mission. They live purposefully with a similar kind of sacrificial, others-centered agenda, which causes them to love with an eternal purpose in mind. The fourth essential of kingdom-designed community is that it is a springboard for living missionally—bringing the good news of Jesus and the kingdom to people in our towns, neighborhoods, and workplaces.

THE MISSION OF GOD

Recall from our discussion in chapter 9 the powerful example of the community of tightly knit men and women who followed close to Jesus. These followers of Jesus were not with Him just for the sake of their own spiritual growth, they were together with Jesus for the sake of a world without hope and without the good news of the kingdom. That community, like every group of friends who gather around the name of Jesus, was purposed not only to follow Him, but to join Him in His mission in our world.

In the early twentieth century, German theologian Karl Hartenstein coined the term *missio Dei* (mission of God) to show that the redemptive, kingdom mission of the body of Christ finds its source in the mission of God. It may come as something of a jolt to realize that redemptive mission is not the idea of the church. Mission is God's idea. David Bosch, author of *Transforming Mission*, writes, "Mission was understood as being derived from the very nature of God. It was thus put in the context of the doctrine of the Trinity."[1] The first community that lived out mission as a foundational characteristic was the community of the Trinity. As we examined in chapter 10, it is in the purpose of God that a watching world observe healthy interdependence in His people, as a reflection of the Trinity. So our view of biblical community finds its source in the community of the Father, Son, and Holy Spirit. Likewise, the mission of God's people is grounded in the mission of God, the Trinity. Though it may seem unusual to put it this way, God, existing in the community of the Trinity, is sent.

In the gospel of John we see repeatedly that the Father *sent* the Son (see John 4:34; 5:24; 8:16; 16:5). In John 4:34, Jesus states His mission as one sent to do the will and the works of the Father. And in the sending of the Holy Spirit, we see the continuation of the ministry of Jesus. In John 15:26, Jesus describes a wonderful picture of the collaborative sending and continued work of redemption among the members of the Trinity: "When the Counselor [Holy Spirit] comes, whom I [Jesus] will send to you from the Father, the Spirit of truth who goes out from the Father, he will testify about me."

It is this collaborative sending activity of God that gives a clear picture of His purposeful energy and mission. Our God is a missionary God. The Father, Son, and Holy Spirit, in community, are involved in a mission. And as we reflect the image of God in our lives, our communities, who find their identity in Jesus, ought to reflect the same purposeful energy and mission. Lesslie Newbigin, in his book *The Household of God*, said that when we consider the community of God's people, its very existence is to be "bearer of that salvation to the whole world."[2]

Craig Van Gelder describes the community of God as, "Missionary by nature, created by the spirit to participate fully in the redemptive reign of God. . . . The sentness of the church is rooted in the apostolic ministry given to the original Twelve. Every community that becomes a part of the church inherits this sentness."[3]

God's people are sent and, in our community expressions, we live out our calling by bringing the hope of Christ to our world. As we consider our personal influence in our world, it happens most powerfully as we join with others in bringing the good news of Christ to our neighborhoods, workplaces, and everywhere we connect with people.

PATRICK'S VISION OF COMMUNITY

In the fifth century, Saint Patrick went to Ireland from England. He had been a slave in Ireland as a young man and sensed God's call to return as a missionary.

Patrick was just sixteen when a band of Irish-Celtic pirates captured him and many other young men, bringing him back to Ireland and selling him into slavery. During his captivity, Patrick came to a deep faith. He also came to understand the culture, language, and heart of the Celtic people. He developed a great love for his captors, hoping that they might come to know God. Through a dream and God's direction, he was set free and returned to England.

At age forty-eight, through another dream, Patrick received God's direction to return to Ireland to bring the Celtic people the gospel. The Celts were barbarians, and most church people didn't see them as worthy of being reached, let alone risking the danger involved in trying. Patrick and his team went to Ireland anyway.

During his days there, among those same barbaric people who had kidnapped him as a boy, he established communities of Christ followers. These communities lived out the gospel message before the people of Ireland, and young men and women who came to faith were equipped for ministry in those same communities. They lived among the Celtic people, educated them, taught them about agriculture, and earned their trust. The difference between the communities grown by Patrick and the religious communities formed by the established church were profound. The traditional, established communities were developed far off the beaten path in an effort to avoid the mayhem of sin-influenced life. And they were composed primarily of priests and monks who were interested in avoiding the riffraff. By contrast, Patrick's Celtic communities were located in the middle of the most crowded and chaotic urban centers of the Celtic world. They were communities led by non-clergy leaders and full of everyday disciples of Jesus. Their purpose was to reach those far from God with the gospel.

During the centuries before Patrick's time, the Roman-led church had begun to assume that the "barbarians" of the north—the Goths, Vandals, Franks, Vikings, and others who wore funny hats—were unreachable. Evangelists of the day gave up and moved on. As a result of that limited thinking, the religious communities of the time became more isolated and insular. During Patrick's lifetime, it is said that as many as seven hundred churches were planted in Ireland. According to scholar and writer George Hunter, in two or three generations, Ireland had become substantially Christian. Because of the work of St. Patrick, Celtic communities became the strategic sending points from which another wave of Christ followers reached the "barbarians" of Scotland and much of Western Europe.[4] All this because a man named Patrick decided to courageously reform Christian community to reflect more fully the incarnation and the mission of God.

BY THIS THEY WILL KNOW

There is only one place in the Bible that Jesus affirms a method of evangelism in one of His prayers. While there are many legitimate means and methods for sharing our faith in Christ, only in John 17 do we find a method sanctioned by the prayer of the Son of God. Just before Jesus is taken to the cross, He prays these words,

> My prayer is not for them alone. I pray also for those who will believe in me through their message, that all of them may be one, Father, just as you are in me and I am in you. May they also be in us so that the world may believe that you have sent me. . . . I in them and you in me. May they be brought to complete unity to let the world know that you sent me and have loved them even as you have loved me. (verses 20-21,23)

Only to the extent that we are together with God and united as believers, will the world acknowledge God's purposes and presence!

As a community of friends on a journey with God, we reflect the character of God most when we embody the unity and love that exists between the Father and Son. Our friends, neighbors, and coworkers will be drawn to Christ when they see love expressed among us in community.

This idea is really just a reiteration of the same principle that Jesus described as a "new command" in John 13 on the night of His last supper with His disciples: "A new command I give you: Love one another. As I have loved you, so you must love one another. By this all men will know that you are my disciples, if you love one another" (verses 34-35).

Our love for one another, in the context of a group of believing friends, is the most powerful way that a community of Christ followers can impact their friends. We'll talk more about this in part 5.

LETTER OF LOVE

When we first moved to Lawrence, Kansas, in the early nineties, we rented a home on a street named Providence Road. During those years, we were blessed with wonderful relationships. Our home was constantly filled with God-seeking friends, including neighbors and college students. Pete and Debra Thompson and their daughter, Michelle, were our neighbors. Michelle was a good friend of our daughters and we spent a lot of time together. The Thompsons were God seekers, but at that time they had not come to know and embrace Jesus. I believe it was the love that they saw in our home and in the community of friends they met in our home that drew them toward Christ. Michelle expressed a desire for Christ first; later Debra came to faith. Some time ago we received this e-mail from Debra:

> I am so encouraged to hear of Jesus moving in your and multitudes of others' lives. And I don't know if I ever thanked you for your witness and prayers for, I would think, me and for my

family in your years here on "Providence." If I haven't, I do so now! Looking back, by His grace I see now see how He gradually worked in my heart. So now I pray that I remember His gracious dealings with me in His timing and sovereignty that I see in Scripture and have personally experienced, so that when He grants me to witness to and pray for others, I will walk in the truth that it is indeed His work, His power, His glory, His timing. And by His grace I plan to pray for you all and His work through you.

God works powerfully through communities of friends as together they hold out the love of Christ. A group of believers that embodies the four characteristics of community we've examined thus far is an attractive and useful group filled with the power and the unlimited capacity of God. This rare and wonderful group will draw people to the Savior. Being a community that joins God in His mission is natural and happens daily as we trust Him.

QUESTIONS FOR REFLECTION

- What lessons about the connection between spiritual community and missional living did you learn about in this chapter? What one lesson could you apply in the next month?
- Identify the primary spiritual community that you are part of. In what ways is that community working together to fulfill the mission of Jesus?

CHAPTER 14

WHOLE-LIFE WORSHIP

The way we worship God is through being involved in radical Christian community.

—TIM KELLER

WE HAD TAKEN a group of students to Haiti to expose them to some of the needs outside their community and to give them the opportunity to love and serve as Christ would. Toward the end of the trip we went to an inexpensive beach resort to debrief with the students before heading home. One Sunday, we gathered for a late afternoon time of sharing, praying, and singing. Several students played their guitars, and we heard from others about the work God had been doing in their hearts during their time in the villages around Cap Haitian and Port au Prince. As our time of prayer concluded, we looked up to see the sun beginning to dip, seeming to almost touch the Caribbean Sea. As it descended, the sun's appearance grew larger and larger. All across the horizon, clouds were streaked with red and orange, then magenta and purple. It seemed God had grabbed His brush and pallet to paint a sunset just for us.

None of us will ever forget that time together. We realized that we had been worshipping and honoring God during each hour of our time among the Haitian people, not just during this very special Sunday evening service.

Tim Keller, in a sermon speaking to the profound difference Jesus made in our definition of worship tells how we glorify God this side of the cross and resurrection of Jesus:

> *Now, the way we worship God is through being involved in radical Christian community. . . . The way that the glory of God shapes us now is not through performances, through rituals, and through observances, but through deep participation in the radically new communal practices — the practices of life together that the grace of God creates amongst people who have experienced His grace. . . . Jesus was continually saying to His disciples "You are a city set on a hill. . . ." You don't worship any more just by going to services.[1]*

The fifth essential of community is just what Keller is describing — 24/7 worship. A worship that flows through every hour of our days and into every relationship of our lives. We're talking about words, actions, thoughts, feelings, and decisions that honor God and reflect Him.

TREASURES OF THE HEART

While the apostle Paul was traveling through Athens he was "greatly distressed to see that the city was full of idols" (Acts 17:16). He said, "Men of Athens! I see that in every way you are very religious. For as I walked around and looked carefully at your objects of worship, I even found an altar with this inscription: TO AN UNKNOWN GOD. Now what you worship as something unknown I am going to proclaim to you" (Acts 17:22-23).

The desire to worship something is part of our human makeup. Just like the Athenians, every person worships something, whether it be a god, a person, or an inanimate object. When Jesus spoke about the things that people put their hope in, He said, "For where your treasure is, there your heart will be also" (Matthew 6:21). Our hearts are inclined to treasure something in life, and each of us can tell stories about different seasons when we were love-struck for a person or thing.

As a college sophomore, I met a young lady during finals week. We studied together, talked, and took our study breaks together. After a couple of days I was love-struck. This young woman had become my treasure. I thought of her most waking hours, tried to be around her constantly, and many decisions in my life began to revolve around her — just as the earth revolves around the sun.

That woman might not be particularly flattered to learn that my crush on her had a lot of similarities to the hobby that was really my first love: fishing. My dad taught me to fish when I was barely able to walk and I have loved to fish ever since. In high school it became more than a hobby, fishing became my treasure — something I worshipped. I was a fanatic. I had subscriptions to a couple of fishing magazines and spent every dollar I could scrape together on fishing poles, reels, and lures. I'd buy topographical maps of our area to hunt down secret ponds and lakes where no one had fished. My time, my energies, my money, and my heart revolved around the pursuit of fish.

We are made to worship something. It might be some religious idol, a person of the opposite sex, a hobby, objects of various kinds, or the God who created the universe and His Son Jesus. The enemy of our souls, the devil, loves for us to worship and honor things, people, experiences, and places rather than giving God Himself the honor and credit He alone deserves. A foundational challenge for the body of Christ in our world today is coming to a full and complete understanding of worship.

EXPANDING THE HORIZONS OF WORSHIP

If it is essential that our community be worshipping, then we better have an accurate understanding of worship. When exactly does worship occur? Am I worshipping when I sing a song in church? When I watch a sunrise? Balance my checkbook? Discipline my two-year-old?

Am I worshipping during an executive team meeting? Worship can happen anywhere and anytime as long as we are living with a desire to honor and glorify God. In Colossians 3:17 Paul gets at this idea, "And whatever you do, whether in word or deed, do it all in the name of the Lord Jesus, giving thanks to God the Father through him." We worship whenever we live to honor Him.

Is a non-believer worshipping when she makes a gift to someone in need? Because they are made in the image of God, even people who don't acknowledge God can bring Him glory and honor as they live out their God-given desires in God-pleasing ways. It doesn't become intentional worship until they consciously act in order to honor and praise God. We'll touch on this more later.

As I've mentioned, I spent my childhood attending church services and came to believe that worship happened in a defined location, on a certain day of the week. After I came to understand the grace of God and began following Christ and reading my Bible, I began to discover that worship was never meant to occur in such a narrow slice of life and experience. While it took many years for this truth to take hold and for those old deceptions to fade away, my world began to expand as I recognized and enjoyed God's presence in the daily pathways of life as well as in more formal worship settings.

I remember once while skiing with some college friends I came to an overlook at Copper Mountain, outside of Denver. As I looked out over those snow-covered mountains my heart leapt. I knew the Creator of those mountains, and that knowledge took my breath away. I gave Him credit for what He has made. We were made to worship. And worship was never meant to be limited.

WHOLE-LIFE WORSHIP

In some religious traditions worship is all about earning God's favor through sacrificing or giving up something of value. Followers of Jesus worship and honor God when *they* become the instruments of worship.

We worship when we live in such a way that God is honored. Romans 12:1-2 says,

> *Therefore, I urge you, brothers, in view of God's mercy, to offer your bodies as living sacrifices, holy and pleasing to God — this is your spiritual act of worship. Do not conform any longer to the pattern of this world, but be transformed by the renewing of your mind. Then you will be able to test and approve what God's will is — his good, pleasing and perfect will.*

This concept is captured in the New Testament by the Greek word *doxa*. This word has a wide range of meanings, but all indicate the idea of glory and honor, anything that exalts the reputation of someone or something. In terms of God it is closely associated with our idea of worship — words or actions that reflect His brilliance and reputation — assigning the highest status to Him.

In 1 Corinthians 10:31 Paul said, "So whether you eat or drink or whatever you do, do it all for the glory of God." Worship is meant to involve all of life, in every use of our body and being, for His glory. Paul captures our increasing ability to glorify God in his words on transformation and change that the Spirit brings in the life of the believer, "And we, who with unveiled faces all reflect the Lord's glory, are being transformed into his likeness with ever-increasing glory, which comes from the Lord, who is the Spirit" (2 Corinthians 3:18). God gets more honor as we grow to reflect Him. Our glorifying God is not reduced to religious activity or things we consider spiritual. Our athletic prowess, verbal abilities, art, music, humor, personal charisma, physical uniqueness, and mental dexterity all are designed to honor Him, whether we end our performance testifying to that fact or not. God has designed us to use every fiber of our personality, gifts, talents, body, and soul to honor Him.

Dallas Willard says of worship, "We embellish, elaborate, and magnify. Poetry and song, color and texture, food and incense, dance and procession are all used to exalt God. . . . In worship we strive for adequate expression of God's greatness."[2] There is nothing that we are or are uniquely gifted to do that, in holiness, cannot be an instrument of praise. And God is not bound to have only believers honor Him.

UNLIKELY SOURCES OF WORSHIP

One day I was reading at our local coffee shop. A friend, Frank, walked in with his wife, Gretchen, and I went over to greet him. Frank is from a religious background, but at this point in his life he was antagonistic toward the Christian faith. We periodically had interesting conversations, as he knew I was a Christ follower. On that day I had made a comment about God blessing people. Frank said that he wanted to bless people's lives. He said he had a family friend whose young child had cancer. Frank's heart was obviously touched as he talked about that family and the hardship they were facing. He went on to describe his desire to serve and help families of children with cancer. He said that he thought God would like it if someday his business would do so well that he'd be able to help those kinds of families with significant financial assistance.

Scripture teaches that though Frank did not have faith in Christ or choose to serve young cancer victims because of biblical motivation, his caring actions are nonetheless worship—because even with his limited understanding, he wanted to honor God's desires. Just as mountains and birds—simply by being mountains and birds (see Psalm 19:1-3; Matthew 6:26)—give praise and honor to our Creator, men made in God's image often bring praise and honor to God by virtue of His creative handprint on their lives (see Psalm 8).

Scripture is full of examples of non-believers bringing honor to God in spite of themselves. Nebuchadnezzar, king of Babylon acknowledged and "praised" the God of Shadrach, Meshach, and Abednego when they were saved from the fiery furnace (see Daniel 3:28). Years later, Cyrus, the king of Persia chose to honor the God of

Israel by allowing a remnant of God's people to return to Jerusalem to rebuild the temple (see Ezra 1:1-4). In doing this, Cyrus fulfilled biblical prophecy and was an instrument of God's purposes and continued fame among His people. God is worshipped whenever, wherever, and by whomever honors Him and increases His fame. Even an occult slave girl was compelled to advertise for the Most High God during Paul and Silas's ministry in Philippi (see Acts 16:16-18). Not exactly the kind of marketing most of us would want!

In the movie *Chariots of Fire*, Eric Liddell describes a similar expanded definition of worship. Family members were questioning the young runner's decision to delay going to the mission field in favor of so worldly an activity as running in the Olympics. Eric told his sister, Jenny, "I believe that God made me for a purpose, for China. But He also made me fast. And when I run, I feel His pleasure. To give it up would be to hold Him in contempt. You were right. It's not just fun. To win is to honor Him."

A PERSON, NOT A PLACE

Worship is not an issue of place or location but is grounded in the object of our worship. Jesus made this clear in His interaction with a Samaritan woman in John 4:19-24. The woman tried to debate Jesus on the proper location for worship—Mount Gerizim, where the Samaritans worshipped, or Jerusalem, the center of Jewish worship—but Jesus would not be distracted. He chose to take the opportunity to teach about the true nature of worship. He said, "Believe me, woman, a time is coming when you will worship the Father neither on this mountain nor in Jerusalem. You Samaritans worship what you do not know; we worship what we do know, for salvation is from the Jews" (John 4:21-22).

Worship is not about *where*. Worship is about *who*. The Samaritans had ceased to worship the Father. Jesus went on to say, "A time is coming and has now come when the true worshipers will worship the

Father in spirit and truth, for they are the kind of worshipers the Father seeks. God is spirit, and his worshipers must worship in spirit and in truth" (John 4:23-24).

If we affirm what Jesus is saying here, we will grow as true worshippers as we gain a clearer and truer view of His greatness; praising and glorifying the Father, the Son, and the Spirit with our hearts, our tongues, and every aspect of our lives.

AN INDWELT PEOPLE, NOT A BUILDING

Certainly, gathering together with other followers of Christ is important and is a form of worship encouraged by God, but showing up at a building every week brings no guarantee that worship will happen. It has been said, "Spending time in a church building is no more a guarantee of someone being a Christian, than spending time in a McDonald's guarantees that a person is a hamburger!"

I grew up believing that frequent church attendance equaled strong religious commitment. I had two friends who reinforced this thinking on a regular basis. If my family was on a trip or if we happened to sleep in on a Sunday, these buddies were sure to deliver a lecture that would leave me with deep feelings of guilt. Participation in a local body of believers is essential to our walk with Christ, but it wasn't until after I began following Jesus and endeavoring to serve Him that I realized that God's view of worship goes further than our weekly attendance at a local fellowship. The presence of the Holy Spirit in our lives is the greatest resource for true worship wherever we find ourselves at a given moment.

The apostle Paul put it succinctly: "Christ in you, the hope of glory" (Colossians 1:27). Our only hope of a life that gives glory to God is a life indwelt by the Spirit of Christ. We *are* His temple and we worship with our whole being because He lives in us. Paul wrote to the Corinthians, "Do you not know that your body is a temple of the Holy Spirit, who is in you, whom you have received from God? You are not your own; you were bought at a price. Therefore honor God with your body" (1 Corinthians 6:19-20).

Paul described the community of Christ followers as the dwelling place of God:

> *Consequently, you are no longer foreigners and aliens, but fellow citizens with God's people and members of God's household, built on the foundation of the apostles and prophets, with Christ Jesus himself as the chief cornerstone. In him the whole building is joined together and rises to become a holy temple in the Lord. And in him you too are being built together to become a dwelling in which God lives by his Spirit.* (Ephesians 2:19-22)

Together, you and I, followers of Jesus, in community, become this "holy temple" as we walk in the Spirit and spread His fame!

GATHERED AND SCATTERED WORSHIP

All this is not to say that a rhythm of gathered worship isn't a priority and a blessing. Hebrews 10:24-25 reminds us of the importance of believers gathering: "And let us consider how we may spur one another on toward love and good deeds. Let us not give up meeting together, as some are in the habit of doing, but let us encourage one another—and all the more as you see the Day approaching." Certainly, a look at the early church in the book of Acts makes it clear that local households of believers came together around teaching, meals, prayer, and sharing life and their possessions (see Acts 2:42-44). God intends for His people to gather together. We honor God when we come together as His people.

This has been true from Old Testament times as well. God went into great detail describing the tabernacle, the place Israel was to gather before the Lord during their wanderings in the wilderness.

He even provided a series of festivals for His people to give them opportunity to remember and give thanks to Him for all He had done from the time they were released from captivity in Egypt to their entry into the Promised Land. Once they made their home in Jerusalem, a temple took the place of the tabernacle. Later, after their exile in Babylon and the destruction of Solomon's temple, synagogues became the gathering place. Along the way, leaders like Hezekiah, Josiah, Ezra, Nehemiah, and Haggai brought the people of God together to celebrate, repent, sacrifice, and remember—to worship and honor Him.

Some of our most meaningful seasons of life have occurred in the context of our local church communities in Denver, Lawrence, and Colorado Springs. The influence of those gathered, whole-life worshippers continues with us to this day. And I have other unforgettable memories of meaningful times of corporate worship. As a young child, I spent many Christmas Eves worshipping with my extended family at midnight Mass amidst the smell of incense, the singing of "Silent Night," and the acknowledgement that a Savior was born in Bethlehem. Prayer and Bible study with our couples small group shortly after we were married taught us the value of intimate venues for worshipping community. I remember the sound of thousands of men singing songs of worship at a Promise Keepers event in the 1990s, in Boulder, Colorado. I can still envision thousands of college students gathered at InterVarsity's Urbana Conference for missions. These are just a few images that portray the value of worshipping God together with other believers.

While our community lives are punctuated by corporate worship, most of our glorifying of God occurs while we are scattered. Thus, we should seek to glorify God in an integrated way in every aspect of our lives. Worship of God, properly defined, is not relegated to certain hours of the week, but is an elevating of God's reputation that occurs constantly. Worship does not revolve around certain holy buildings or sites, but it has been revolutionized by the Holy Spirit who indwells us and, together in community, makes us His temple. God has equipped us to worship Him in every season of life, at every moment, and with every aspect of our being.

Jean Vanier, in his book *Community and Growth*, describes kingdom community this way: "It is a place of resurrection, a current of life: one heart, one soul, one spirit. It is people, very different one from another, who love each other and who are all reaching towards the same hope and celebrating the same love."[3] Whole-life worship is expressed in those small, daily encounters where we choose to have each of our relationships display love, hope, and celebration as recipients of God's grace.

The community that God desires us to experience is one characterized by interdependence, authenticity, transformed lives, joining God's mission, and honoring Him through lives of integrated worship. May God give us the grace to experience this kind of community and to help others experience it as well.

QUESTIONS FOR REFLECTION

- What places or activities cause you to spontaneously praise God or honor Him with your words, actions, or thoughts?
- What new ideas about worship and glorifying God stand out to you from this chapter? How will these thoughts change how you view worship or your involvement in honoring God?
- Are there ways your spiritual community could grow in its involvement in whole-life worship?

PART 4

NA PALI COAST

*Where His Waves Transform Us
to Reflect His Goodness*

CHAPTER 15

LIFE IN THE GAP

And we, who with unveiled faces all reflect the Lord's glory, are being transformed into his likeness with ever-increasing glory.

— PAUL (2 CORINTHIANS 3:18)

PAM AND I celebrated our twenty-fifth anniversary on the island of Kauai in Hawaii. It had been Pam's dream to go to Hawaii ever since our attempts to spend our honeymoon there fell through many years ago. During our trip, we had the opportunity to go on a boat tour of the Na Pali Coast, on the western shoreline of the island.

Like all the Hawaiian Islands, Kauai was formed by a volcano. It is basically a big chunk of volcanic basalt that has surfaced in the Pacific Ocean. Over the centuries the ultra-hard igneous rock has crumbled, making way for the lush vegetation that makes the island the tropical paradise it is today. The striking and beautiful shoreline was formed over the years by winds, repetitive tides, and unrelenting waves, carving the Na Pali Coast into an intricate series of cliffs, archways, and caves. The area is a photographer's dream.

God is molding and shaping us in much the same way. Some habits, character ruts, and sins are like the seemingly unbreakable basalt rock of Kauai. In past chapters I've described times when I looked in the mirror and wondered if I was ever going to change. But God is committed to seeing us through the transformation process.

First John 3:2 helps us know that we can be sure that when we meet Jesus face to face, the transformation will be complete: "But friends, that's exactly who we are: children of God. And that's only the beginning. Who knows how we'll end up! What we know is that when Christ is openly revealed, we'll see him—and in seeing him, become like him" (MSG). At times God uses subtle tides and winds to shape us and at other times crashing waves break and form the basalt of our souls. We can be sure that as God fashions us, turning our hardness into tropical lushness, we will become like Him.

As our lives are transformed, they become postcards for the watching world. When others see in us the image of Christ and our increasing freedom from the chains that bind us God uses us as waves of grace, wooing people who need the same transformation and the same deliverance. Sadly, though, pollsters report that those who profess to be Christians often live lives demonstrating the same level of morality or lack of morality as those who do not profess to be Christians. Without a doubt, this poses a great integrity challenge for the body of Christ. We need to become people who reflect the change that Christ brings. The answer to the dilemma is Christ followers who join God in His plan to change them and thus portray the difference that Jesus can make in our lives, families, and communities.

THE THEOLOGY OF CHANGE

The idea of transformation describes what theologians call *sanctification*, the process where followers of Christ become holy, pure, and set apart for the purposes of God. Billy Graham, in his book *The Holy Spirit*, describes three aspects of sanctification:

> First, *the moment you receive Christ there is an immediate sanctification. Second, as we progress in the Christian life there is a "progressive sanctification." Third, when we go to*

heaven there will be total and "complete" sanctification, which is called "glorification." [1]

It is the second "progressive" aspect of sanctification to which I refer when I mention God's transforming work in our lives.

This work of transformation is accomplished by the three Persons of the Trinity: the Father, Son, and Holy Spirit. The Father purposed and is the source of our redemption. He put in motion the plan of salvation in His Son Jesus. The Son sustains us and is the means of our transformation. Jesus Christ's death on the cross redeems us and makes it possible for us to experience new life. The Holy Spirit applies the transforming purposes of the Father and the work of the Son to those who follow Christ. The Spirit is the means of new life, renewal, and transformation. Chapter 18 will discuss in more detail the Holy Spirit's involvement in transformation.

God jealously and graciously transforms us, causing us to bend and be reshaped as His new creation. Sometimes it's painful, but often the pain is forgotten as we see Him increasingly reflected in our lives and enjoy the glory He is producing in us.

I remember when our kids were little, periodically we would catch them dressing up like mom or dad. One time, I caught one of our daughters looking in the mirror and mimicking some actions that she had seen Pam do recently. This little one was working very hard to make sure she captured every nuance of her mom's style. On my dresser I have a picture of myself standing next to my son, Will. We are side by side in bath towels, right after a shower. Will was so proud that day, standing as tall as a three-year-old can stand, certain and proud that he was just like his dad. As little children, we aspire to live up to our parents' desires and to grow to become like them. God has wired us to reflect our parents. This is even more true regarding our destiny to reflect our heavenly Father and His Son Jesus. The Greek word *metamorphoo*, found in 2 Corinthians 3:18 — "And we, who with unveiled faces all reflect the Lord's glory, are being *transformed* into his likeness with ever-increasing glory" (emphasis added)—describes the process of progressive change. We were made to reflect God's image, and we do so increasingly as we join the Spirit in His work. The promise that we can take to heart is that the Lord will not cease until He has finished the job of transforming us.

RESCUED FROM DESPAIR

At times we wonder if God can change us. We look at the course of our lives and wonder at the mess we've made of it. *What can God do with this!?*

The movie *Seabiscuit* is an incredible story of redemption and transformation. A business owner's world is rocked by the tragic death of his son and the Great Depression. On the backside of those forming waves, he gets into horseracing and becomes the main character in the story. The man's unlikely success story revolves around a dubious group of characters: a horse that is too small, a washed-out trainer, and a jockey who is too big. All three of these characters have had tough lives filled with defeat. They are far from revealing the full potential they were designed to reflect. As the story progresses each of them begins to grow, change, and move closer to reflecting that potential.

One of the lines in the movie that communicates this underlying transformational theme happens when Charles (the owner) sits with the trainer, Tom Smith, to get to know him. They have a conversation about an injured horse. When Charles hears that even if the horse recovers she'll only be a cart horse or show pony, and that she will never race, he asks Tom, "Why are you fixing her then?" Tom replies, "You don't throw a whole life away just 'cause he's banged up a little bit."[2]

There is a wonderful truth in that statement, a truth also found deeply embedded in the gospel message. God will not simply throw away lives that are banged up and battered by sin. Those of us who put our hope and trust in Jesus Christ—no matter how banged up and battered we may be—have hope that God will redeem, restore, and transform us.

The seven portraits of spiritual death listed in chapter 8 characterize people living apart from Christ. It is a dismal list that reflects so much of the futility and hopelessness we recognize in people estranged from God. It is not God's intent for us to remain in that pit of despair. God desires to transform us. These seven portraits of life are hope-filled new realities in the life of a believer:

1. No longer estranged from God, but **reconciled** (see Romans 5:10).
2. No longer enslaved by desires that do not please God, but **set free** (see Romans 6:18).
3. No longer without hope, but **hope-filled** in Christ (see Romans 15:4-6).
4. No longer citizens of darkness, but **citizens of the kingdom of the Son** (see Colossians 1:13).
5. No longer hopeless in broken relationships, but **growing in reconciliation and unity** (see Galatians 3:28).
6. No longer blind to spiritual things, but **enlightened by the Spirit** (see 1 Corinthians 2:9-15).
7. No longer deserving judgment, but by grace **receiving eternal life** (see Romans 6:23).

We have great hope in Christ, because God is committed to restoring His people to the image of His Son. Andrew Murray, in his book *Humility*, gives this encouragement:

Let us study the Bible portrait of the most humble man that ever lived — the Lord Jesus. And let us ask our brethren, and the world, whether they recognize in us the likeness to the original. Let us be content with nothing less than taking each of these texts as the promise of what God will work in us, as

the revelation of what the Spirit of Jesus will put within us.
Allow each failure and shortcoming to only the more quickly
turn us to the meek and lowly Lamb of God in the assurance
that where He is enthroned in the heart, His humility and
gentleness will be the streams of living water that flow from
within us.[3]

In a world where many professing Christians live lives that are no different than the non-believing world, these truths are critically important. The spotlight is on the promise that God made in the Old Testament, pointing to transformed lives, aligned with the Spirit of God, "I will give you a new heart and put a new spirit in you; I will remove from you your heart of stone and give you a heart of flesh. And I will put my Spirit in you and move you to follow my decrees and be careful to keep my laws" (Ezekiel 36:26-27).

LIVING BETWEEN THE NOW AND THE NOT YET

It would be very easy to believe that if only we had the same opportunity that Jesus' closest followers had—being with Him personally and benefitting from that direct and tangible interaction—surely our tendency toward fickleness and faithlessness would fade away and we would be changed men and women. Wouldn't we be transformed and increase in faith if we had *that* chance?

There they were, packed in the boat together, the disciples and Jesus. Leaving the throngs of people behind, they headed across the Sea of Galilee (see Mark 4:35-41). Their restful day was short-lived, however. In the middle of their journey a squall came up and the waves tumbled over the sides of the boat. The sky turned dark and the storm's intensity put fear even into the hearts of these sturdy fishermen. They hoped for the best, not wanting to wake Jesus as He slept in the front of the boat. Finally their fear got the best of them:

"Jesus, wake up! Don't you care that we are about to drown?" Jesus drowsily came out of His slumber and rest, looked around, and sat up. He spoke to the waves and wind, "Quiet! Be still!" In an instant the wind died down and everything was quiet. The disciples were dumbfounded and embarrassed. They had seen Him heal, cast out demons, and teach with great authority. *Why had they not been at peace?*

Jesus finished rebuking the waves and turned His rebuke to His doubting friends: "Why are you so afraid? Do you still have no faith?" Unfortunately, we can relate all too well. Yes, even those privileged to be in His physical presence struggled the same way we do. We're living between the now and the not yet. Our life in relationship with Christ is a life that is most often two steps forward and one step back. We live between the vision and assurance of what we are becoming and the stark reality of our sin, doubts, reactions, and missteps. Yet we are assured of being transformed. At times we do see it and are amazed that we are changing.

John Ortberg, in his book *The Me I Want to Be*, speaks of the *gaps* that the gospel is meant to overcome. At the beginning of our life with God, we are aware of a gap between God and us, a separation from God because of sin. Ortberg goes on to confirm that even after we come to faith in Christ and begin to follow Him, "there is still a gap. Now the gap is between the me I am right now and the me I'm meant to be — 'current me' and 'sanctified me.'"[4]

As we begin part 4, considering the topic of transformation and God's purposes in our lives, it is essential we understand that God doesn't throw a life away just because it's banged up a little. We are all banged up and we all live life in the gap between who we are now and who God is making us. Even Jesus' closest disciples struggled with lack of faith and sin. We take hope knowing that God is committed to finish the job He has begun. In the next chapter, we'll consider three mainstays God values as we grow and are transformed.

QUESTIONS FOR REFLECTION

- Look at the list of the seven portraits of life in this chapter. Which of these hopeful statements means the most to you as you reflect on it? Pray and thank God that this is true of you as a follower of Jesus.
- As you live between now and when we see Jesus face to face, what "gaps" do you see in your life—areas in which you want to grow? Bring those areas before Jesus and ask Him to walk with you in them.

CHAPTER 16

THREE PILLARS OF LIFE IN CHRIST

And now these three remain: faith, hope and love.

— PAUL (1 CORINTHIANS 13:13)

IN MANY URBAN U.S. neighborhoods it is common for people to buy homes only to tear them down and build new, more expensive homes. Rather than preserving and restoring the property, it makes more economic sense to bulldoze the house and start over. It's only every once in a while that a developer will see the potential of the old house and go to the extra effort to preserve the history and build on the foundational attributes that made the home attractive through many years. We're fortunate that our God is into restoration not demolition. God's preference is transformation, taking who and what we are and making us into something beautiful. He is in the business of bringing beauty out of ashes and restoring us to become reflections of Himself. As we consider life between the now and the not yet, we have great assurance that Jesus is not done with us and that He has promised to finish His transforming work.

A thorough study of the life of Christ and a good reading of the letters of the apostle Paul leave no doubt that certain character traits represent God's vision for our transformation. There were three words that Paul often used to characterize that life. And indeed, these same traits find emphasis when we watch Jesus' interaction with people, especially His disciples. If we were to ask God for just three things that would typify our lives as He shapes us into an imitation of Christ, what would they be? Consider these introductory words from Paul's letter to the Colossians:

> *We always thank God, the Father of our Lord Jesus Christ, when we pray for you, because we have heard of your faith in Christ Jesus and of the love you have for all the saints — the faith and love that spring from the hope that is stored up for you in heaven and that you have already heard about in the word of truth, the gospel that has come to you.* (1:3-6)

In this passage of Scripture, there is a wonderful relationship among three attributes that Paul commends the saints for. They are faith, love, and hope. As we work through these characteristics, consider your own life. What work needs to be done in these areas in your soul remodel?

WITHOUT FAITH, IT'S IMPOSSIBLE

Faith ranked high in Jesus' estimation. Along with love, faith was the thing Jesus looked for most in His followers. Faith was certainly something others saw in the lives of Jesus' followers. In Matthew 8:5-8, a Roman military leader came to Jesus one day and appealed to Him to heal his paralyzed and suffering servant. Jesus offered to go to the house where the servant was resting and heal him. But the centurion told Jesus this was unnecessary, and basically said, "There's no need for you to come." "I'm not deserving of your presence in my home, and besides, I know you have the authority to do it from here." Jesus responds in astonishment and says to those following Him: "I tell you the truth, I have not found anyone in Israel with such great faith" (Matthew 8:10). Jesus was amazed at the faith and action of this non-religious, non-Jewish man. Evidently, it takes more than religious or spiritual behavior to impress Jesus, it takes placing confidence in God when it matters most.

Faith is a major theme of the book of Hebrews. It is defined there as "being sure of what we hope for and certain of what we do not see" (Hebrews 11:1). Without faith, we are hopeless, for "without faith it is impossible to please God, because anyone who comes to him must believe that he exists and that he rewards those who earnestly seek him" (Hebrews 11:6). But, like all aspects of our life in Christ, it's easier to talk about than it is to live.

Pam and I had been married several months when we learned of a new church beginning in south Denver. We both had jobs and were managing an apartment building near downtown that provided us with free rent and a small salary. A couple of months later, the people starting the church asked us to consider helping by launching the youth ministry. As we prayed and sought counsel, God made it clear that we should say yes and serve, using the vision and skills He had given us during our college years. One thing stood in the way, however; it was not a paid position. Further, because the church was starting in south Denver, we felt we were too far away to connect fully with the junior high and high school students we'd be working with. Most of them lived and attended schools thirty to fifty minutes from our current apartment.

Leaving our apartment management role would mean giving up a big part of our income, and we would have nowhere to live. We looked into getting an apartment at the graduate school I was attending, but there were no openings. We were stuck. We knew faith was important, but moving forward without these answers seemed foolish.

Nevertheless, we became increasingly convinced that this was something God wanted us to do. We began to pray that God would confirm this by providing us with a job and a place to live. It was December and we hoped to make the move by March. We took comfort in the example of Abraham's faith in the face of dire circumstances, described in Romans 4:19-21:

> *Without weakening in his faith, he faced the fact that his body was as good as dead—since he was about a hundred years old—and that Sarah's womb was also dead. Yet he did not waver through unbelief regarding the promise of God, but was strengthened in his faith and gave glory to God, being fully persuaded that God had power to do what he had promised.*

Just as with Abraham, God came through for us in what seemed a crazy and surprising way! In a Christmas card to the man who had sold me Pam's wedding rings, I half-jokingly offered that I'd be willing to sell diamonds for him there in Denver. He called when he got the card, and the next thing I knew I was on my way to establishing my own jewelry business. The job would be paid purely on commission, but the net was exactly what we needed. Pam continued her job and I sold enough jewelry to provide most of the income we needed to work in the youth ministry. The rest of our needed funds came in through house-sitting and providing childcare for families in the church. God did immeasurably more than we asked or imagined during that time. We even earned a little extra income and never lacked for a place to live.

Christian faith is not faith in faith. It's not wishful or positive thinking. It's not faith in ourselves. The important dimension of true faith is the One in whom we have faith. And faith does act. It is not passive. The assurance and unwavering aspect of faith is seen in our actions—our willingness to move forward despite uncertainty or our courage to wait patiently for God to show us the way forward.

ALL GOD'S COMMANDS IN ONE WORD

No one spent much time with Jesus without hearing about and seeing love in action. If anyone knew the love of Jesus firsthand and wrote about it with great vividness, it was the apostle John. Interestingly, he was known as the disciple Jesus loved (see John 20:2). Certainly, it was his conviction that Jesus was God in the flesh and his firsthand experience of Jesus' love for him that caused him to write, "Whoever does not love does not know God, because God is love" (1 John 4:8).

Jesus put love at the top of the list of character traits for kingdom citizens. He said, "A new command I give you: Love one another. As I have loved you, so you must love one another. By this all men will know that you are my disciples, if you love one another" (John 13:34-35). Love is the distinguishing trait of His disciples. To be a follower and learner of Jesus is to be a person of love. When asked His opinion regarding which commandment is greatest, Jesus answered that love for God is first, followed by love for neighbors.

The apostle Paul also considered love the synthesis of God's commands — "The entire law is summed up in a single command: 'Love your neighbor as yourself'" (Galatians 5:14).

A few chapters back, I told about the discipleship and training program I attended my first year out of college. Rich Beach, the founder of Doulos Ministries, was a good friend and mentor. He later officiated at our wedding, spoke at my ordination service, and spoke at my mother's funeral.

On one occasion during my year at Doulos, four of us had gone into town and were on our way back to the house where we were living. Rich and I were in my mighty, four-squirrel-powered little Ford Fiesta. We followed the other two guys in their little Fiat. The guys in front were racing a bit, showing off the little sports car. Just outside of town, we came to a turn onto a gravel road. Rich, apparently tired of putzing along, said, "Nunk, take them at the corner! They'll go high on the turn and you go low."

My normally conservative nature was suddenly infused with a dose of adrenaline. I took Rich's advice and assumed the personality of Jimmy Johnson. We cut the corner, left our friends in the dust, and flew down the gravel road with them in hot pursuit. The Ozark Mountain roads are filled with hairpin turns and steep inclines, but somehow my little Ford-that-could stayed in the lead all the way to our destination. They were still behind us and my heart was pumping hard when we reached our gravel driveway!

As we approached the driveway, which was framed by two stone pillars, I began to realize that the good judgment I had left back on the main road was now needed. Adrenaline would not help me turn the corner into the driveway. Too late, I began to apply the brake. The wheels locked up and we went into a slide right into a stone post. All we really saw in the Fiat as it passed us were the enormous smiles of the two passengers. I climbed out of the car to examine the crushed front end.

I had no money to spare to fix that car. Each of us had committed to this year-long discipleship program and agreed to do it almost as volunteers. Even if I could have skipped buying groceries for a month, the two hundred dollars I got for a stipend was not nearly enough to get the car fixed. As Rich and I pushed my gimpy car up the driveway toward the house, Rich said words I'll never forget, "Nunk, call Harvey's Car Repair in town, have them fix it, and I'll pay for it." While there's no doubt that Rich was an accomplice to my misfortune, it was I who made each choice along the way; it was I who was behind the wheel the whole time; it was I who missed the turn; and it was I who owned the car.

Rich was a man who loved people. He took seriously Jesus' call to love in John 13:34-35. He modeled for me, as a young man, a spirit of giving, serving, and loving that I had not experienced before. Through my life, I had learned that you had to look out for yourself, and if you were going to make it, you needed to focus on protecting, competing, and moving yourself forward. Rich showed us through his life that God's intent for Christ followers is a life of love for both fellow believers and for those yet to know Him.

HOPE THAT TRANSFORMS

While our world may equate hope to wishful thinking or optimism, biblical hope is confident expectation based on what God has said He has done or will do. Kingdom hope points us to the future. Hopeful Christ followers handle their present reality in a fundamentally different way because of what God has said. Hope informs convictions we have of what will be true in our future, whether that be tomorrow, in twenty years, or in eternity.

Far from a contrived emotional state that we whip up anytime we are feeling down, hope can be a powerful force in the life of every believer. Hope is one of the characteristics developed through the transformation process.

Here are some characteristics of biblical hope.

First, biblical hope is grounded in Jesus Christ. Hear the apostle from Tarsus's greeting to his ministry partner, Timothy: "Paul, an apostle of Christ Jesus by the command of God our Savior and of Christ Jesus our hope" (1 Timothy 1:1). Christ, not some temporal future possibility, is our ultimate hope. Because of that, our hope cannot disappoint, though every earthly hope ultimately will.

Second, biblical hope has its inception in the new birth and eternal life we have in Jesus Christ. Peter and Paul both echo this in their letters:

Praise be to the God and Father of our Lord Jesus Christ! In his great mercy he has given us new birth into a living hope through the resurrection of Jesus Christ from the dead. (1 Peter 1:3)

He saved us through the washing of rebirth and renewal by the Holy Spirit, whom he poured out on us generously through Jesus Christ our Savior, so that, having been justified by his grace, we might become heirs having the hope of eternal life. (Titus 3:5-7)

Recall from our look at Ephesians 2 how we were without hope in the world. Our new life in Christ has changed all that. This is not some kind of mind game. It's a present reality that flows out of our new identity as children of God in Christ.

Third, biblical hope is in the promise of our ultimate transformation when we meet Jesus face to face. The apostle John described this in 1 John: "But we know that when he appears, we shall be like him, for we shall see him as he is. Everyone who has this hope in him purifies himself, just as he is pure" (3:2-3). As God's children, we have confidence that when we see Jesus we will finally and fully experience our completed transformation. This is the hope that causes us to give ourselves to Him fully, to depend on Him to transform us, and to know that this will produce in us the purity of Christ.

Fourth, our growth in faith and love emanates from biblical hope. Recall again that key phrase from Colossians 1:5, "the faith and love that spring from the hope that is stored up for you in heaven and that you have already heard about in the word of truth, the gospel." Our hope is the wellspring of biblical faith and love. The future hope we have is in an eternal relationship with God and in the promise that God will complete in us what He has promised. Again, our hope in Christ is not just hope in hope or hope in positive thinking. Biblical hope is grounded in the God who made the heavens and earth. It grows in proportion to our ability to completely trust what He has said. Hebrews 10:23 says, "Let us hold unswervingly to the hope we profess, for he who promised is faithful." Our hope is built on God and His faithful promises.

The hope we have in Christ gives us confidence for the future, no matter what we are facing. We have hope in our eternal destiny because Christ died for our sins. We have hope in our final transformation, because He promises to form us into the likeness of Christ, and we have hope because we are children of the King of kings and Creator of the universe.

OUR FUTURE IN HIS HANDS

My junior year of college I had a chance for a stipend in my social work curriculum. Because I was paying my own way through college, this meant that my university would provide a certain amount of money for my education. The only condition was that I would need to enter employment with a government-based job after graduation to pay back the grant. I went through the whole process of application, believing that there was no other way I could afford to finish out school without the help the stipend would provide.

The week before my final interview with the deans of the arts and sciences department, I was praying and the Spirit of God challenged me. *Was I sure that He was leading me to take a government job after graduation? Did I believe that God could provide in some other way?* I had already been wondering if there was some kind of short-term ministry opportunity God would have me join after graduation, but I had put that out of my mind because of my financial worries. After a few days praying, I came to the conviction that God wanted me to keep my future, and my hope, in His hands. He wanted me to keep my options open for what He had for me and to trust Him to provide for me financially.

I went into my interview and told them why I needed to withdraw my name from consideration. I gave testimony to Jesus' lordship in my life and explained how I knew that I needed to keep my options open to His direction for my life after graduation. I felt good knowing that I had the opportunity to talk about my spiritual convictions with those men and women. Some of them may have thought I was foolish, but who knows how my hope in God may have affected them?

What I knew was that I needed to put my *hope* in the God who had rescued me and who promised He would take care of me. And He did. He provided other means of financing my education through part-time jobs and a great summer job. As I look back on how my life unfolded after that pivotal point, I clearly see God's hand. First came the ministry internship I did with Rich Beach, which I described earlier. Guidance I received that year directed me toward marrying Pam. Friendships in that small group of men still sustain and encourage me. I can scarcely imagine how different the trajectory of my life might have been had I not put my hope in God for that financial provision. The ripple effect of my hope in Christ has been far-reaching.

When we consider what a transformed life is meant to look like, there is little doubt that faith, love, and hope are mainstays for the life of Christ followers. And these three are key products of the transforming work of God in our lives. It is God's desire that our walk with Him would result in increasing evidence of each of these spiritual commodities. While each of us is living between the reality of our current life, with all its warts and weaknesses, and the future promise of an increasingly Christlike character, we can live with confidence that God will change us so that we will honor Him more fully.

QUESTIONS FOR REFLECTION

- Is there an area of life that is currently stretching you and in which you would like to see your faith increased? Pray and ask God to help you in your unbelief.
- Is there a particular person you could love in a tangible way this next week? Who is that person and what could you do to love him or her?

CHAPTER 17

SO YOU WANT TO BE LIKE JESUS

And being found in appearance as a man, he humbled himself and became obedient to death — even death on a cross!

— PAUL (PHILIPPIANS 2:8)

OVER THE PAST several years, my passion for fly-fishing has caused me to develop an interest in bugs. The entomology of the stream — the understanding of midges, mayflies, and caddis flies is part of the well-taught fly fisherman's body of knowledge. One interesting fact is that stream-born insects do not stay as they are born. Most begin life as worm-like creatures on the bottom of the stream, writhing in the current and often falling easy prey to lurking trout. Their journey to adulthood climaxes when they finally emerge from running waters in the form of a wonderfully transformed winged creation of the type that is often featured on the covers of fly-fishing books and magazines. Remarkably colored and decked out with sparkling, translucent wings and long, upright tail fibers, their lift-off from the stream is a beautiful sight — if they manage to make it past the mouths of waiting fish!

The metamorphosis of the nymph to the adult mayfly is an example of God's transformative work, not unlike what He promises for His children. Our part in God's change process is to imitate Jesus' model for life. Just as His efforts and focus were on living out the will of His Father, not just professing it, we emulate Jesus' way of living, we partner with Him in suffering, and we empty ourselves on behalf of others. These are three essential and challenging steps for becoming more like Him.

A NEW MODEL FOR LIVING

It was just another day for Jesus. He spoke out in public and the religious leaders challenged Him, struggling with who He claimed to be. The Feast of Tabernacles had just ended. The focus of that celebration had been God's faithfulness during Israel's wandering years in the wilderness after their release from Egyptian captivity. The symbols of water and light were prevalent, bringing to mind God's provision of water in the desert and the pillar of fire that guided them by night. Coming at that moment in time, Jesus' claim, "I am the light of the world" (John 8:12), was not coincidental and caused the Pharisees to explode with accusations and questions, "Who are you?" (John 8:25).

Jesus' answer provides a first essential step for us who seek to be like Him. To answer their question regarding His identity, Jesus began speaking of His heavenly Father, who sent Him. But the Pharisees were confused and did not understand that He was talking about God, His Father (see John 8:26-27). Jesus clarified His identity, saying, "When you have lifted up the Son of Man, then you will know that I am the one I claim to be and that I do nothing on my own but speak just what the Father has taught me. The one who sent me is with me; he has not left me alone, for I always do what pleases him" (John 8:28-29).

Jesus understood His own identity through the one who sent Him. Because Jesus was sent by His Father He was to represent Him and to mirror His purposes in our world. Similarly, we are to find our identity and way of living through Christ, because He is the one who sends *us*. Speaking of His united purpose with the Father, Jesus said,

- "I do nothing on My own." — Jesus does the **works** of the Father (see John 4:34).
- "I speak just what the Father has taught Me." — Jesus speaks the **words** of the Father (see John 14:24).
- "The one who sent Me is with Me." — Jesus was always **with** the Father (see John 16:32).
- "I always do what pleases Him." — Jesus does the **will** of the Father (see John 6:38).

Just as Jesus does the works, speaks the words, is with, and does the will of the Father, becoming like Jesus will mean that we are increasingly doing His works, speaking His words, living out His desires, and experiencing more and more what it means to be with Him. Jesus' words silenced the Pharisees and caused many to put their faith in Him. To the extent we live in the same way, our lives will reflect the undeniable presence of God and those around us will see Him in us.

PARTNERS WITH HIM IN PAIN AND SUFFERING

A second essential step in becoming more like Christ is to recognize that suffering is something He experienced, and it is a normal part of the life of a Christ follower. The apostle Paul, testifying of His desire to know Christ and be like Him said, "I gave up all that inferior stuff so I could know Christ personally, experience his resurrection power, be a partner in his suffering, and go all the way with him to death itself" (Philippians 3:10, MSG).

Being like Jesus means viewing suffering and pain as part of life. The Scriptures teach that Jesus' suffering was an instrument of learning. Hebrews 5:7-8 says,

During the days of Jesus' life on earth, he offered up prayers and petitions with loud cries and tears to the one who could

save him from death, and he was heard because of his reverent submission. Although he was a son, he learned obedience from what he suffered.

This is not saying that Jesus was ever disobedient, but that through suffering Jesus experienced the deep lessons regarding obedience that are learned only through submission to God and His ways.

As Christ followers we experience an even greater benefit of suffering. We not only learn obedience through suffering with Christ, but our suffering and trials in this world also refine us. Hardships are one of the key ways that God breaks us and molds us to be like Christ.

In C. S. Lewis's book *The Voyage of the Dawn Treader*, we see a great metaphor highlighting the place of pain in our transformation. In this tale, Lucy and Edmund, two of the main characters from other Narnia adventures, have found their way back into Narnia. This time their obnoxious cousin Eustace has stumbled in with them. During the adventure, they travel by ship and come to an island inhabited by a dragon. Having wandered off by himself, Eustace finds the dragon dying and ends up being driven by a rainstorm into the dragon's lair. Once inside, he finds himself atop a huge pile of treasure—and is quickly dreaming of all the ways he could use this newfound wealth! Exhausted from his day's adventure, and unable to leave the cave because of the rain, he falls asleep atop the treasure pile. When he awakes, something terrible has changed, and he has a horrifying revelation: "He had turned into a dragon while he was asleep. Sleeping on a dragon's hoard with greedy, dragonish thoughts in his heart, he had become a dragon himself."[1]

Eustace's coveting becomes an insightful metaphor of our human condition. We are all beasts of some sort, all of us at times struggling with and embodying the deeds of the flesh (see Galatians 5:19-21). We need help. Eustace's unfortunate mutation comes with many fears and future misfortunes. Eustace becomes broken and his heart turns to a place of repentance. The boy no longer wants to be like a dragon! It is at this point that Eustace has a life-altering experience with Aslan the lion, the Christ figure of the Narnia series.

Aslan tells Eustace that in order to become a boy again he needs to bathe in a special pool, and before he bathes he must first "undress" (rid himself of the scaly dragon skin). Eustace tries to undress himself, but each time he rips and tears at himself, trying painfully to shed his scaly skin, he finds that there is one more layer underneath. Time after time, he tries, always with the same result. He remains a dragon. It is at this point that Aslan speaks to Eustace, telling him that he would have to undress him. Here Lewis portrays the connection between suffering and transformation,

> *I was afraid of his claws, I can tell you, but I was pretty nearly desperate now. So I just lay flat down on my back to let him do it. The very first tear he made was so deep that I thought it had gone right into my heart. And when he began pulling the skin off, it hurt worse than anything I've ever felt. The only thing that made me able to bear it was just the pleasure of feeling the stuff peel off. . . . Well, he peeled the beastly stuff right off . . . and there was I as smooth and soft as a peeled switch and smaller than I had been. Then he caught hold of me — I didn't like that much for I was very tender underneath now that I'd no skin on — and threw me into the water. . . . I'd turned into a boy again. . . . After a bit the lion took me out and dressed me . . . in new clothes — the same I've got on now.[2]*

What a wonderful metaphor of how God uses pain and suffering to teach us and transform us. Our partnership in His suffering creates a fellowship between us and Jesus. As we submit and seek to live under His guidance, He causes us to become more like Himself.

Consider the words from the servant song in Isaiah 53. They vividly portray the suffering of the Messiah.

But the fact is, it was our pains he carried —
   our disfigurements, all the things wrong with us.
We thought he brought it on himself,
   that God was punishing him for his own failures.
But it was our sins that did that to him,
   that ripped and tore and crushed him — our sins!
He took the punishment, and that made us whole.
   Through his bruises we get healed.
We're all like sheep who've wandered off and gotten lost.
   We've all done our own thing, gone our own way.
And God has piled all our sins, everything we've done wrong,
   on him, on him.
He was beaten, he was tortured,
   but he didn't say a word.
Like a lamb taken to be slaughtered
   and like a sheep being sheared,
   he took it all in silence.
Justice miscarried, and he was led off —
   and did anyone really know what was happening?
He died without a thought for his own welfare,
   beaten bloody for the sins of my people. (verses 4-8, MSG)

In this beautiful passage, we see the benefits we receive as a result of His suffering. From the beginning of time, it was ordained that Christ would suffer. All who come into relationship with Him are recipients of the grace provided through His suffering. Our willingness to submit to Him and enter into pain-filled places offers us the opportunity to serve a needy world and gives us the chance to grow to be more like Him.

EMPTYING OURSELVES

In our early years of marriage, Pam and I struggled with repetitive, ongoing disagreements and arguments. This was one of the areas of life that kept showing us that we *did not* have our act together. There were tears, raised voices, and great frustration. As is often true, the real issues were not the topics about which we fought. The real issues we needed badly to address were various aspects of our own sinful hearts. One of the breakthrough discoveries for me was when I understood that I did not really know how to live out my wedding vows, those promises I had so confidently and naively confessed many years before. Something about loving my wife as Christ loved the church (see Ephesians 5:25) was proving to be a bit of a challenge.

I now view that sacred oath that I uttered standing before many friends a little differently. Essentially, I was committing that in my marriage I was going to be like Jesus. Clearly, as a twenty-three-year-old, I had no idea what that meant. And in my vows I didn't pay real attention to the phrase at the end of Ephesians 5:25: "and gave himself up for her." The way Jesus loves is a self-denying, sacrificial love that does not live for itself, but for others.

In Philippians 2:5-8, we see this concept even more vividly:

Your attitude should be the same as that of Christ Jesus:

> *Who, being in very nature God,*
> *did not consider equality with God*
> *something to be grasped.*
> *but made himself nothing,*
> *taking the very nature of a servant,*
> *being made in human likeness.*
> *And being found in appearance as a man,*
> *he humbled himself*
> *and became obedient to death —*
> *even death on a cross!*

These verses summarize the spirit of Jesus' life and death:

- He gave up His rights, rather than hanging on to His divine privileges.
- He made himself nothing, emptying Himself, rather than taking full advantage of His divine power.
- He chose to serve, rather than to be served.
- He humbled Himself and died for us, rather than asserting His own authority.

So we who follow Jesus must also learn to empty ourselves and live for others. This is a third essential and sobering truth for those who want to become like Him. Becoming like Him means not asserting our rights and prerogatives. Rather, we are to humbly and sacrificially serve those God brings into our lives. We don't need to wonder, as the popular spiritual slogan "What Would Jesus Do? (WWJD)" suggests. Instead we can move forward in confidence, walking according to the model God has given us in Christ's submission to the Father, willing to suffer with an attitude of humble servanthood. Consider the eternal influence Christ had, and then consider what He may do through you as you follow in His steps. Solomon describes such a transforming path in Proverbs 4:18: "The path of the righteous is like the first gleam of dawn, shining ever brighter till the full light of day."

QUESTIONS FOR REFLECTION

- When you think about a life modeled after Jesus Christ, what are ways you could have your words be more like His words, your actions and interactions with others be more like His, and overall please Him more fully?
- Is there some relationship or challenging situation in your life right now in which you might need to give up your rights and serve the other person?

CHAPTER 18

THE SPIRIT OF GOD AND HIS SCALPEL

We should never divorce the Spirit of God from the Word of God.

— JERRY BRIDGES

AS A COLLEGE student, I studied social work. I had grown up in an upper middle class home and was attending a school that had a high tuition, so most of my classmates had grown up in similar or more affluent homes than I had. Most of the schools I had attended up to that point had insulated me from many of the needs in the world. During my days studying and practicing social work, I came face to face with the injustices and inequities that exist in our American culture. I was convicted of my own sin and callousness toward people who are oppressed and living in poverty, people who have been painfully impacted, through the generations, by systems of injustice.

Alongside my class studies, I also studied the Scriptures to discover God's view of poverty, corruption, and injustice. I began a journey of transformation in terms of those areas of my life, and I continue to ask God to change me more. Each of us has areas of life where we need to change and where we need to trust the Spirit to transform us.

These many changes will not take place by human effort. God has provided powerful resources to bring about the transformation He has promised and purposed. And Scripture promises His commitment to making our life one that honors and reflects Him.

The work of the gospel in the life of the believer means an ongoing transformation of our mind, attitude, and lifestyle. What means does God use to transform us into the image of Christ? Chapter 12 spoke of the influence of community in the transformation process. The role of relationships is clearly one of the instruments God uses to change us into His likeness. However, when we consider the primary catalyst for transformation, it is the work of the Holy Spirit and the Spirit's scalpel, the Word of God. It is a compelling study to examine how the Spirit of God works in tandem with the Word of God.

TAG-TEAM TRANSFORMATION

At a recent conference I attended, Jerry Bridges spoke. In his comments about spiritual transformation, he said, "We should never divorce the Spirit of God from the Word of God." The Holy Spirit is God and is one of three persons in the Trinity. The Word of God should never be considered His equal. However, it is interesting to see the synergy between the Spirit and the Word. Consider these remarkable examples:

1. At the creation of the world "the Spirit of God was hovering over the waters" (Genesis 1:2), even as God spoke everything into existence. The author of Hebrews reiterates: "the universe was formed at God's command" (11:3).
2. At the baptism of Jesus "the Holy Spirit descended on him in bodily form like a dove. And a voice came from heaven: 'You are my Son, whom I love; with you I am well pleased'" (Luke 3:22). Here again we see the powerful partnership of the Spirit and the Word.

3. At Jesus' temptation we see Christ "full of the Holy Spirit" as He "returned from the Jordan and was led by the Spirit in the desert" (Luke 4:1). As He faced the temptations of the devil, He had the Word of God on his lips (see Luke 4:3-12).

4. In His Old Testament promises regarding inward change, God guarantees transformation through putting a new Spirit in us (see Ezekiel 36:26-27) and placing His law within us (see Jeremiah 31:33).

5. At the point at which we are born again (see John 3:5), we are saved by the washing of rebirth and renewal by the Holy Spirit (see Titus 3:5), and this is accomplished "through the living and enduring word of God" (1 Peter 1:23).

Furthermore, the Bible shows an interesting connection between having Christ's Word in us and being filled by the Holy Spirit, which is the power for a life of following Jesus. Note the parallel between Colossians 3:16: "Let the word of Christ dwell in you richly as you teach and admonish one another with all wisdom, and as you sing psalms, hymns and spiritual songs with gratitude in your hearts to God" and Ephesians 5:18-19: "Do not get drunk on wine, which leads to debauchery. Instead, be filled with the Spirit. Speak to one another with psalms, hymns and spiritual songs. Sing and make music in your heart to the Lord." These two passages show the similar effect of having God's Word stored up in our hearts and the filling of the Holy Spirit, both providing help we need to live in joyful obedience.

Ephesians 6:11 describes the "whole armor of God" (ESV), His divine gear for those who believe. Verse 17 describes a key piece of this spiritual equipment: "Take the helmet of salvation and the sword of the Spirit, which is the word of God." Here we see clearly that God's Word is an instrument used by the Spirit, and it is in fact the one offensive weapon in our arsenal.

Even the way the Word of God was produced gives evidence to

the Spirit's purposeful involvement with the Scriptures. The Word of God is:

- Spirit produced (see 2 Peter 1:20-21; Acts 28:25)
- Spirit taught and echoed (see John 14:26)
- Spirit revealed (see 1 Corinthians 2:12-14)

Numerous times during my life the Spirit of God has used the Scriptures to convict me of areas in my life that need change. As a young believer, I was convicted of how I sinned when I gossiped about my friends and the dire consequences of that behavior, as "a gossip separates close friends" (Proverbs 16:28). Just a year later, as I was spending a lot of time with a girlfriend who was not yet a believer, the Spirit got my attention and helped me to bring some needed distance in that friendship, for "It is God's will that you should be sanctified: that you should avoid sexual immorality" (1 Thessalonians 4:3). Recently, when I was finding my significance and security in accomplishments and man's applause, the Spirit reminded me with the example of Paul, who said, "May I never boast except in the cross of our Lord Jesus Christ" (Galatians 6:14). Through the years, when I found myself seeking life purpose through working hard and performing, the Spirit of God said, "My soul finds rest in God alone; my salvation comes from him" (Psalm 62:1) and "In repentance and rest is your salvation, in quietness and trust is your strength" (Isaiah 30:15). The Spirit's transforming work in my life through the Word of God is a consistent, ongoing activity.

The Word of God is a powerful instrument the Spirit uses in the lives of believers to form us into the character of Jesus. Everyone who desires to follow Jesus is wise to spend time in the Word of God and to be sensitive to the Spirit's guidance and direction through the Word.

THE SCALPEL OF THE SPIRIT

As I described in the last section, trusting the Holy Spirit to speak through the Word of God is not for the faint at heart! If we truly long to become holy, set apart and growing in Christlikeness, we must expect the Holy Spirit to challenge us and do surgery. Consider the description of the power and invasiveness of the Word,

> *For the word of God is living and active. Sharper than any double-edged sword, it penetrates even to dividing soul and spirit, joints and marrow; it judges the thoughts and attitudes of the heart. Nothing in all creation is hidden from God's sight. Everything is uncovered and laid bare before the eyes of him to whom we must give account.* (Hebrews 4:12-13)

What makes the Word of God alive and active is that it has power to touch our hearts. The Holy Spirit uses it to penetrate deeply into our souls. The Word of God has the ability to rightly judge our thoughts and attitudes. We are held accountable to God through the Word, and God's view of us is full and unblocked. He sees it all! Our lives, actions, thoughts, and attitudes are right there for Him to see. Truly, God's Word is a scalpel in the skillful hand of the Spirit.

The many instances where God got my attention through the Word would not have happened if I were not spending time in the Scriptures. The Navigators have developed the illustration of a hand to describe the importance of God's Word. The hand includes five ways believers can learn from the Scriptures: hearing, reading, studying, memorizing, and meditating. With the advent of computer-generated presentations, I find that most believers don't even take their Bibles to church anymore. Because the Bible shows up on a screen, we may be vulnerable to lose a generation of Bible-loving Christ followers. I wonder how many believers still have a reading and study plan for their lives. I will only comment briefly here on the importance of memorization and meditation as it relates to the Spirit's work of transformation. (An expanded explanation of the Hand illustration can be found in appendix A.)

Psalm 119:9-11 says, "How can a young man keep his way pure? By living according to your word. I seek you with all my heart; do not let me stray from your commands. I have hidden your word in my heart that I might not sin against you." As we commit portions of Scripture to memory, whether a verse or a chapter, it becomes part of our soul software. It begins to reorient our thinking, feeling, and deciding. As the psalmist says, it helps us to make our way pure — working to transform us into the image of Christ.

Having the Word stored in our hearts enables the Holy Spirit to use those words and helps us live under their direction. This is the transforming influence of memorized Scripture. Further, having the Scriptures memorized provides us with God's truth, ready to be shared with whomever we might encounter during the day, whether someone yet to know Christ or another believer in need of a good word. Proverbs 22:17-18 says, "Pay attention and listen to the sayings of the wise; apply your heart to what I teach, for it is pleasing when you keep them in your heart and have all of them ready on your lips."

Just this morning I was meeting with a younger follower of Christ. As we went over a topic we had agreed to talk about, the Lord brought a few extra verses out of my mental storehouse that I was able to share with him. If I had not memorized those passages, they would not have been there for the Holy Spirit to use. (The Navigators has a great Scripture memory course called the *Topical Memory System*, which can be found at www.NavPress.com.)

Meditation is the chewing or ruminating on God's Word. To ruminate means to casually or slowly go over something in your mind repeatedly and often. In the animal kingdom, there are animals called ruminants, like cows and deer, which have multiple stomachs. These animals digest their food by holding it in their first stomach, called the rumen, and then passing it back up to the mouth to be chewed again and again. The word *ruminant* comes from the Latin *ruminare*, which means "to chew over again." When we meditate on Scripture, that is actually what we are doing—chewing on it and thinking about it again. Through this means, God's Spirit takes the verses and helps us to apply them to our lives, thus changing our hearts and actions. Jim Downing, one of the first Navigators, said, "Just as a ruminant animal extracts nourishment from grass or hay through chewing and transferring it into its bloodstream, so also as we meditate on the Word of God we extract the life of Christ and transfer that life into our spiritual bloodstreams."[1]

THE WORK OF THE SPIRIT

Without a doubt, the most oft-forgotten member of the Trinity is the Holy Spirit, yet our transformation will not occur without His work. When we consider the Holy Spirit's transforming work in the life of each believer, four key aspects of His work need to be emphasized.

First, it is the Holy Spirit that makes us a new creation. When we decide to follow Christ, it is evidence of the fact that God's Spirit has brought about a new birth (see John 3:3-8). The promised Holy Spirit indwells each believer (see John 14:17). Eugene Petersen, in his book *Christ Plays in Ten Thousand Places*, speaks of the Spirit's work both in the first creation, where God breathes life into Adam, who becomes a living soul; and the second creation, where God breathes life into us, re-creating us, just as He did His disciples in the first century (see John 20:22). The beginning of our transformation is the new birth, and it is just the beginning of the Spirit's masterpiece.[2]

Second, the Spirit of God is holy and is involved in making us holy. In Romans 1:4 the Holy Spirit is described as the "Spirit of holiness." The Greek word for *holy* means set apart. For instance, we have a plate in our home that is red and gilded around the edge are the words "You are special." That plate is holy. It is set aside for a special purpose—being used only for special occasions, such as birthdays. Those who have been given new birth by His Spirit are reserved for

His purposes. Through the transforming work of the Spirit we are increasingly holy, increasingly set apart for the purposes of God.

Third, the Spirit teaches and guides believers into fuller understanding and application of the ways of God. I sometimes wonder what it would be like to have Jesus right here teaching and guiding me in life. Well, He knew that we would think that! In fact, right before He died, rose from the dead, and ascended into heaven, He anticipated that desire. He said, "I have much more to say to you, more than you can now bear. But when he, the Spirit of truth, comes, he will guide you into all truth" (John 16:12-13). Jesus also said, "But the Counselor, the Holy Spirit, whom the Father will send in my name, will teach you all things and will remind you of everything I have said to you" (John 14:26). The Spirit works to guide and direct our lives in line with the teaching and words of Jesus.

Finally, the Spirit produces fruit and gifts in our lives. The fruit of the Spirit, as described in Galatians 5, are character traits produced by the Spirit that reveal the Spirit of Jesus. We can tell whether we are experiencing the transforming influence of the Spirit to the extent that we see these fruit in our lives. You can tell an apple tree because it produces apples; an orange tree because of the oranges on its limbs; and a fig tree because it bears figs. Someone under the influence of the Spirit will bear spiritual fruit: "love, joy, peace, patience, kindness, goodness, faithfulness, gentleness and self-control" (Galatians 5:22-23). In addition, the Scriptures teach us that He gives gifts to each believer, meaning certain spiritually inspired abilities that allow us to be involved in serving and loving other people so that they too can benefit from the Spirit's work in their own lives (see Ephesians 4:7-13; 1 Corinthians 12; 1 Peter 4:8-11).

NO LONGER TRAPPED IN CONFORMITY

In the movie *A Beautiful Mind*, Russell Crowe plays John Nash, the Nobel Prize mathematician. It is the story of a man with an incredible mind. During the first half of the movie, we are introduced to Nash and his friends. We soon discover that Nash's mind was a complex cage in which he was trapped. Certainly, the mind is a mysterious thing. At times, even in healthy people, the mind seems to take on a life of its own. The New Testament concept of the mind reflects a broader idea than just a person's intellect. In Paul's writings, the mind is synonymous with the heart or the soul. These words describe the entire inner man, not just the intellect. To Paul, the idea of mind or heart portrays who we are on the inside—our thinking, our feelings, and our will.

God's plan for spiritual growth and transformation revolves around the transforming renewal of the mind, not leaving us in some kind of trap of empty reasoning, delusions, or worldly thoughts. In Romans 12:2, Paul writes, "Do not conform any longer to the pattern of this world, but be transformed by the renewing of your mind." God's work of spiritual transformation is focused on the metamorphosis of our hearts and minds. This release from captivity, this change of heart and mind, happens through the Holy Spirit and the Word of God. What a phenomenal gift. God has by His Spirit made us a new creation, and has given us the ability to live according to His purposes and principles found in the Scriptures. Through these means, God's influence on our lives can reach beyond us to a hurting world.

QUESTIONS FOR REFLECTION

- Is there some way that the Scriptures have been challenging you to be more like Christ? Maybe it's a passage of Scripture you've read in this book. What is God asking you to do?
- Is there an area of life in which the Spirit of God is showing you your need for growth? Find a Bible verse relating to that area of life and commit it to memory.

CHAPTER 19

WHO DO YOU THINK YOU ARE?

You can tell for sure that you are now fully adopted as his own children because God sent the Spirit of his Son into our lives crying out, "Papa! Father!"

— PAUL (GALATIANS 4:6, MSG)

ONE SUMMER IN my high school years a friend invited me up to his family's cabin on Lake Chautauqua in New York state. Early in the morning, Tim and I took a canoe out onto the lake to go fishing. Lake Chautauqua was home to the wily, mean-spirited Muskie, the largest freshwater game species in the United States. Muskies are a dream catch for any angler. They can grow to more than fifty inches long and more than fifty pounds. They are hard to catch and their gaping mouths are filled with hundreds of sharp teeth.

Earlier that morning, I had seen a large Muskie cruising just beneath the surface of the lake. He was gliding around just beyond where I could cast one of the small lures I was using. As we launched the canoe, we put Tim's little sister, whom we were babysitting, in the center, and we quickly saw that monster Muskie again. I threw my lure out in front of him and to my surprise that forty-inch torpedo gobbled it! After a good twenty-five minute fight, I was able to get that trophy up close to the boat. My buddy Tom grabbed the only net we had available: a tiny trout net. As I reeled the fish in alongside the canoe, Tom tried his best to net him. However as soon as that little net touched the fish, there was a mid-air explosion. In a silver flash, that angry fish, my lure, and my line were history! Losing that fish was probably not a bad ending to the story, because Tim's sister would definitely not have appreciated that toothy critter's company in the canoe!

In some lakes, Muskies breed in the same location as another type of large fish, the Northern Pike. Because the two are distinct species, this doesn't work out so well. When the eggs and sperm of these two species get intermixed, the offspring are a hybrid known as Tiger Muskie. Neither Muskie nor Northern Pike, Tiger Muskies have an identity problem. They have a short life span and they cannot reproduce.

In the body of Christ many people are a little like those Tiger Muskies. They take on part of their identity in Christ, but hold on to other attributes of life without Christ. Because of this duplicity, they lack a clear and unified sense of their true identity. They tend to pick and choose behaviors, merging sin patterns with churchgoing or other religious activities. Our enemy, the devil—with the help of media, advertising, and our success/beauty/superstar culture—shouts at us, trying to convince us to aspire to take on various false identities:

- "Unless you drive a car like _____, you are a second-class citizen."
- "Men will only like you if you look like _____."
- "Your job is what defines you as a person."
- "You are part of the 'in crowd' if your kid is the star of the team."
- "Sex is what life is about; loosen up and go for it."
- "What you wear makes you who you are, so spend, spend, spend because life is short."

These are only a few of the messages hurled at us on a daily basis. Is it any surprise that we are confused about who we are and how God views us? Believers who fall deeply into chasing these kinds of false identities are similar to the Tiger Muskie. They lack a single, clear identity; they lack staying power, and they are spiritually infertile. Others of us, like me as a young believer, really want to assume the identity of a new creature in Christ, but the lies we have come to believe are hard to shake, and we struggle to experience the freedom and joy meant for Christ followers.

I've shared a number of stories through the pages of this book that relate to challenging events in my life. These events shaped my life primarily through how I began to view myself as a result of those experiences. For instance:

- *I moved nine times before graduating from high school.* Through that experience and the challenge of making new friends in each new community, I began to believe that I was always on the outside looking in. I felt like an outsider, just beyond the fringe of each relational circle. This misperception impacts me even today when I enter a new situation.
- *I was a late bloomer.* Because I spent junior high and most of high school as the shortest guy, I came to believe that I needed to try a little harder in order to survive or be recognized. This led to the belief that performing and succeeding were the keys to my identity. It is a false belief and a form of legalism to find life in performance.
- *I lived to perform.* My mom and dad held high standards for me growing up, both at home and at school. I learned some very good lessons and developed a healthy ability to work hard. I also came to believe the lie that my self-worth was dependent on how I performed. I can still struggle with a need to be right or do right.

Of course, all these ideas are lies about who I am. They are false beliefs that can impact my emotions, decisions, and actions. Often, difficult or traumatic events convince us of viewpoints that are not really true. We begin to believe these lies and actually live our lives based on them, rather than on our identity in Christ.

God means for each of us to leave behind distorted views and have a new view of ourselves based on the truth of Scripture. Our sins, wounds, and limitations lead us to broken dependence before God, but God does not leave us broken. Scripture has much to say on how we are to view ourselves!

CHECK YOUR ID

Most mornings, before I ever get out of bed, I review five truths that help me remember the new identity that characterizes my life as a follower of Christ. These quiet moments are probably the most important time of my day. Before my brain has a chance to play the soundtrack of lies I can believe about myself, and before the enemy can step in to confirm this litany of false identities, I must call to mind what God says about me in His Word. A number of years ago, my friend Sid Huston shared with me an acrostic—C. R. O. W. N.—that helps me remember how God sees me.[1] It provides a lens through which we can see with a new freshness how God loves us and views us as His own.

- C—*Christ* is our life.
- R—God sees us as *righteous* and pleasing in His sight.
- O—We are citizens of a new *order,* the kingdom of Jesus Christ.
- W—We are *worshippers* of the one true King.
- N—We are *nobility;* the King has adopted us as His princes and princesses with all the rights of heirs.

As I've reflected on these five truths over the years, here are some of what the Spirit of God has taught me.

C — Christ Is Our Life

Many things vie for supremacy in our lives. People, jobs, things, and dreams attempt to take the throne of our life. Paul's words in Colossians 3 capture our true identity in Christ. Here it is in *The Message*,

> *Your old life is dead. Your new life, which is your real life — even though invisible to spectators — is with Christ in God. He is your life. When Christ (your real life, remember) shows up again on this earth, you'll show up, too — the real you, the glorious you. Meanwhile, be content with obscurity, like Christ.* (verses 3-4)

When we are thinking with the mind of Christ, we consider our old way of life dead and gone and we embrace the new fact that Jesus Christ *is* our life. He doesn't just provide life to us, or provide good things for our lives — He is our life! Our daily lives revolve around our relationship with Him.

R — Righteous in Christ

As I've mentioned, I grew up learning a deep sense of responsibility and probably believed the statement, "God helps those who help themselves." As you've probably already figured out, a more biblical edition of that phrase is "God helps those who see their need for help." Nevertheless, I grew up believing that if anything was going to happen, I needed to expend the effort to get it done. Rather than understanding the concept of grace, I continued to try to earn God's favor through working hard, doing my best, and performing. It wasn't till some years later that I discovered that "righteousness" could not in any way be achieved by human effort. Only God could provide me with righteousness through Christ. I still struggle to fully experience and live out of that truth.

Through His death on the cross, Jesus took upon Himself our sins, making us righteous (see 1 Peter 2:24). The apostle Paul eloquently summed it up this way: "God made him who had no sin to be sin for us, so that in him we might become the righteousness of God" (2 Corinthians 5:21).

Most of us, when we consider God's view of us, assume that He must be pretty disappointed. We imagine His glaring eyes fixed on our shortcomings and failings. Not true! Because Jesus took our sins upon Himself when He died on the cross, God sees us washed clean and righteous before Him. This process is what theology calls justification. Recently, Jerry Bridges told me that justification means that "we have been showered clean of our sins and clothed with righteousness. We stand before God as if we've never sinned and as if we have always obeyed." It's still hard for me to fully believe that God views me this way, but it is true. This certainly gives deeper meaning to the term amazing grace!

O — Citizens of a New Order

In 1991, because of the change of relations between the former Soviet Union and the United States, then U.S. President George Bush gave a speech to the congress describing a "New World Order," a system whereby nations working together would usher in a new reality. The word "order" referred to a system and quality of authority giving leadership and rule to the world. As believers, we often use the word "kingdom" to describe the same concept. Obviously, we don't need to go much further than the daily news report to see that chaos continues to reign around the world. In this world, ruling orders or kingdoms come and go. However, in the life of each believer, this idea of kingdom is an important and powerful one.

In his letter to the Colossians, Paul summarizes this idea with great clarity, "For he has rescued us from the dominion of darkness and brought us into the kingdom of the Son he loves, in whom we have redemption, the forgiveness of sins" (1:13-14).

When I ask Christ followers what they believe it means to be "saved" or rescued by God, the most common response is that one who is saved has eternal life and heaven guaranteed. While that is wonderfully true, the rescue of God has many other life-altering implications! One is that, through the redemption of Christ, we have been rescued from the dominion (authority) of darkness and transferred to a new kingdom of the Son. This is a groundbreaking concept. When I awaken each morning I am able to remind myself that I no longer answer to the call of darkness. Instead I serve the good, loving, gracious, sacrificial, and powerful king Jesus. Just as there are different cultures across national boundaries, the cultural differences between the kingdom of light and the kingdom of darkness are a stark contrast. Each day, I remember that my spiritual driver's license says "Citizen of Jesus' Kingdom." My identity as His subject comes with freedom, privilege, resources, and responsibility. It is so important to remember that the One we bow to as king is Jesus Christ.

W — Worshippers of the King

The fourth truth that orients my life each day and reflects my identity as a new creature in Christ is that I am a worshipper of the one true King. As we discussed in chapter 14, we are designed for worship. Our personal default mode is to honor, worship, or idolize someone, or something. We glorify and exalt something in our life each minute that we breathe. The question is, What object of worship do we exalt?

In Deuteronomy, Moses reminded the children of Israel of who deserves our worship. After reminding them of how God brought them out of Egypt he said, "Acknowledge and take to heart this day that the LORD is God in heaven above and on the earth below. There is no other" (4:39). As people of the one true God who rules over the heavens and the earth, we worship Him alone. There is no other.

N — Nobility of the Kingdom

Our king Jesus has chosen to call us His children. Soak up these words in Paul's letter to the Galatians from *The Message*,

You can tell for sure that you are now fully adopted as his own children because God sent the Spirit of his Son into our lives crying out, "Papa! Father!" Doesn't that privilege of intimate conversation with God make it plain that you are not a slave, but a child? And if you are a child, you're also an heir, with complete access to the inheritance. (4:6-7)

This final crowning aspect of our identity overwhelms and humbles me. Consider that God not only saves us from our sins and makes us righteous but He also makes us His own sons and daughters. We are heirs: princes and princesses of the King of kings. My adoption as a child of God is an incredible truth that ought to change the way I live each day of my life. God sent His Spirit into my life and it is His Spirit that prompts us to cry out, "Papa! Father!" The word *Abba*, used in most translations is the Aramaic word Jesus, as a small child, would have used to call to Joseph, and later to His heavenly Father.

Seeing myself as a son of a heavenly Father who loves me and cares for me is the most heart-changing truth for me personally. The fact that I can literally cry out to God, "Papa!" helps me understand the love of the Father and the kind of relationship God wants to have with me. As I've gone through difficult aspects of life—like my mother's death and my father's cancer—my ability to endure and hope can only be explained by the access I have to my "Abba."

The second part of this passage in Galatians 4 is equally remarkable. Because we are His children, we are also heirs and therefore have access to God's inheritance. In one of his letters, the apostle Peter wrote that "His divine power has given us everything we need for life and godliness through our knowledge of him who called us by his own glory and goodness" (2 Peter 1:3). Because we are His children and His heirs, God has made available *everything we need for life and godliness.* Everything!

KINGDOM CITIZENS

Aren't these truths incredible? The work of the Spirit in our life transforms us by giving us each a new identity, an image that reflects our new standing as His kingdom citizens. In Paul's letter to the Corinthians he wrote, "So from now on we regard no one from a worldly point of view. . . . Therefore, if anyone is in Christ, he is a new creation; the old has gone, the new has come!" (2 Corinthians 5:16-17).

Because of this new relationship with Christ and the resulting new birth, our view of one another changes, as well. We stop viewing one another primarily in worldly terms of race, social status, wealth, and titles. Instead we view one another through the truth of our new identity in Jesus. The good news of Christ promises us a new way of seeing ourselves, and that, in turn, yields a new way of living in and influencing this world.

With these great truths ringing in our ears, we move on to the practical matter of living this out. We are to live out faith with boldness and risk in a desperately needy world that is largely "without hope and without God" (Ephesians 2:12). The full picture of transformation includes addressing the question, "Because of all that God has done in our lives, how are we to live in a world that needs the hope of Christ?"

QUESTIONS FOR REFLECTION

- Review the C. R. O. W. N. verses that tell us about our true identity in Christ. Which of them do you need to remember most today? Pray and thank God for these truths.
- Are there ways you tend to view yourself that are not true from God's perspective? Ask God to replace these lies with His truth.

CHAPTER 20

TRANSFORMATION AS REVOLUTION

The main measure of your devotion to God is not your devotional life, it is simply your life.

— JOHN ORTBERG

THE GOSPEL IS supposed to create a revolution — a total and radical change — in the lives of men and women. Our faith is not just about securing a place in heaven but about giving us the power of Christ to live as an influence for His kingdom in our present hurting world.

Frustrated with the inaction of many in the Christian subculture, our current generation has begun participating widely in issues of culture and justice. They hunger for the authenticity that comes when life and beliefs or professions and actions align.

Our oldest daughter, a social worker, and her husband are interested in seeing their faith lived out in how they influence and change their world for the kingdom of God. Our middle daughter currently works at a faith-based human rights organization and serves weekly at a local homeless shelter. Our son has a passion for serving others and is quick to lend or give money away to those in need.

This type of revolution is a natural outpouring from lives changed by Jesus. They are compelled to move beyond words to action.

WOE TO HYPOCRITES

One can easily observe that some of the tension between Jesus and the religious leaders of His day was heightened by the fact that the religious leaders seemed to be largely removed from and callous to the needs of people around them. It was obvious what Jesus thought:

> *The teachers of the law and the Pharisees sit in Moses' seat. So you must obey them and do everything they tell you. But do not do what they do, for they do not practice what they preach.* (Matthew 23:2-3)

> *Woe to you, teachers of the law and Pharisees, you hypocrites! You give a tenth of your spices — mint, dill and cummin. But you have neglected the more important matters of the law — justice, mercy and faithfulness.* (Matthew 23:23)

Railings like these are representative of Jesus' unflagging insistence on integrity and practicing what we preach. Not too long after pronouncing these woes on the Pharisees, Jesus told the parable of the sheep and the goats recorded in Matthew 25:31-46. This was pointed directly at the hypocritical religious leaders and trumpeted a clear standard of loving behavior required of those who follow Him. We are to feed the hungry, give drink to the thirsty, clothe those needing something to wear, look after the sick, and visit the prisoners.

John Ortberg states this succinctly: "The main measure of your devotion to God is not your devotional life, it is simply your life."[1] The world is not impressed with our religious activities or our devotional activity, no matter how genuine and fervent. Jesus calls us to have faith that makes a difference in life, such that the revolution in our own souls works its way outward to a broken humanity.

TELOS AND PRAXIS

Researchers and pollsters tell us again and again that the values and actions of those who claim connection to church and to Christ are not much different than those who lack these relationships and affiliations. This reality may be at the heart of why many people are increasingly disinterested in church and Christianity. Unfortunately, Jesus often gets a bad name because of the lack of integrity of His followers.

Steven Garber, in his book *Fabric of Faithfulness*, asks the question, "Do you have a *telos* sufficient, personally and publicly, to orient your *praxis* over the course of your life?"[2] By *telos* Garber means life purpose or ultimate goal and by *praxis* he is describing how we really live. He's asking us in essence, "Is your stated life's purpose sufficient to cause you to live a life that displays with integrity and power the truths that you profess?" In the course of his explanation, Garber makes reference to Walker Percy's warning about people "getting all A's but flunking life."[3] Does that describe you, as it did the Pharisees of Jesus' day?

The body of Christ, in certain places and at certain times in history, has received an A on doctrine, while failing miserably in their testimony to a watching world. Conversely, the entire life of Jesus is a practical display of faith in action. Without a doubt, Jesus took to heart the words of the prophet Micah: "He has showed you, O man, what is good. And what does the LORD require of you? To act justly and to love mercy and to walk humbly with your God" (Micah 6:8).

And James, the brother of Jesus and leader of the Jerusalem church, knew well the heart of Jesus on these matters. In his letter, he exhorts us not to allow ourselves to live in a way that does not reflect our faith:

> But be doers of the word, and not hearers only, deceiving your-selves. (1:22, ESV)

> What good is it, my brothers, if someone says he has faith but does not have works? Can that faith save him? If a brother or

sister is poorly clothed and lacking in daily food, and one of you says to them, "Go in peace, be warmed and filled," without giving them the things needed for the body, what good is that? So also faith by itself, if it does not have works, is dead. (2:14-17, ESV)

By its very definition, Christian discipleship means living in the way that Jesus lived. And as we saw in chapter 17, being like Jesus means living a life of service, selflessness, and love for neighbors.

Vernon Grounds, who served as dean, president, and then chancellor of Denver Seminary, bemoans in his booklet *Evangelicalism and Social Responsibility*, the tendency of Christ followers to be theologically astute, but absent from places in the world where they are needed most. He writes,

It is imperative, then, that as evangelicals we engage in some hard thinking about our social responsibility. Are we faithfully obeying God's will as it has been disclosed in God's Word? Are we communicating and implementing a full-orbed gospel? Is our version of Christianity truncated, perhaps emasculated, and therefore something far less than the dynamic it ought to be? Are we reading the Bible through the dark glasses of tradition, failing to see what it actually teaches and how it actually bears upon every dimension of life? [4]

ACCEPTABLE WORSHIP

Pastor Tim Keller helped me make an important connection in my understanding of social outreach and engagement.[5] The writer of Hebrews ends chapter 12 with a strong admonition to worship: "Therefore, since we are receiving a kingdom that cannot be shaken, let us be thankful, and so worship God acceptably with reverence and awe, for our 'God is a consuming fire'" (Hebrews 12:28-29).

While most Old Testament worship was comprised of religious ritual on certain days and during festivals, New Testament followers of Jesus are destined to worship with words, actions, thoughts, and feelings 24/7. The first three verses of Hebrews 13 go on to describe the worship that God expects from us as followers of the Lord Jesus:

> *Keep on loving each other as brothers. Do not forget to entertain strangers, for by so doing some people have entertained angels without knowing it. Remember those in prison as if you were their fellow prisoners, and those who are mistreated as if you yourselves were suffering.*

How do we worship God acceptably, with reverence and awe? We endeavor to love one another as brothers and sisters, we entertain strangers, and we care for prisoners and the mistreated. What a remarkable connection the Scripture is making here! Perhaps this is the exhortation we need to move us to live out a revolution in our own world.

LIVES OF RISK AND SUBVERSION

Rodney Clapp, in his book *A Peculiar People*, suggests that the church should engender a culture of its own, living out a different kind of life in the midst of a world needing the gospel. He coins the term "sanctified subversion." Subversion means to undermine the power and authority of an established system or institution. Clapp suggests that when we read the Bible as strangers and aliens in this world, its pages explode with examples of sanctified subversion.[6] It seems that, rather than live revolutionary lives, many believers make peace with a world system that is antagonistic to faith and the values of Jesus.

During college, Pam and I were involved in leading a student fellowship group that was very active on campus. We were engaged in the dorms, active in sharing our faith and engaging in friendship with people yet to know Christ. During those years, we saw many friends move toward Jesus, and some of them came to follow Him. We were helping fellow students learn how to live out life in Christ among their friends, so there were many students sharing the good news in deed and speech. One day I received a phone call from a campus administrator, asking me to come into his office. I had no idea why he would want to talk with me, but it seemed serious.

A couple of days later I went into the administrator's office. He was disturbed with what was going on with our fellowship group, and particularly that we were sharing the gospel through our network of friends all over campus. He suggested that we were acting a little zealous and wanted us to tone things down a bit. I was respectful, but as I left the office I was excited. I felt that I had just experienced a bite-sized taste of what Peter and John had experienced when confronted by the religious leaders of the first century. Our little fellowship group was committed to take risks and to put our faith in action. We were living lives of "sanctified subversion," and through us, Jesus was changing our little corner of the world.

WORLD CHANGERS

The transforming work of the gospel makes us more like Jesus. This means that we are not involved in a religious club that passively sits around and ponders the tenets of faith; rather, we are active in living our faith and trusting God to use us to change our world.

History is full of people who lived subversively for the sake of Christ. Biblical examples include Moses, Daniel, Esther, and Nehemiah, to name a few. Others include St. Francis, St. Patrick, Count Nicholas Von Zinzendorf, William Carey, Martin Luther, Ignatius Loyola, Mother Teresa, Martin Luther King, and Billy Graham. Let me share the stories of three others who God used to change the world for the honor of Christ: William Wilberforce, the Moravians, and Rosemarie Haefeli.

William Wilberforce, a member of the British parliament in the late 1700s, is well known for his twenty-year battle and eventual success in eradicating the slave trade in England. Wilberforce was a follower of Christ whose life purpose was revealed to Him through prayer. In his journal he wrote, "God Almighty has set before me two great objects: the suppression of the slave trade and the reformation of manners." By "reformation of manners" Wilberforce meant that he was to be a force for redefining what was considered moral. Slave trade was one thing that was considered moral at the time. According to Bob Beltz and Walt Kallastad in their book *World Changers,* Wilberforce didn't cease following this life purpose after winning the slavery battle, but spent thirty additional years working as an instrument of the kingdom. Beltz says, "Wilberforce either started or helped to fund 69 different societies that targeted almost every social and cultural issue of his day. Societies against the use of child labor, societies to provide medical care for the indigent, a Bible society, missions societies, a national gallery of art—he took on everything."[7]

In the early to mid eighteenth century, a movement known as the Moravians was birthed in the areas of Europe known as Bohemia and Moravia. John Huss founded the first church that ended up growing into a prolific missionary movement. The Moravians' zeal was motivated by the sacrifice of the Lamb of God—Jesus. They felt that they walked in the footsteps of Jesus when they sacrificially took the gospel to the poor and marginalized, though they brought the message of Christ to people in all parts of society. Throughout Europe, these Christ-lovers established communities of people who were committed to the Scriptures and to living them out. They were committed to living a lifestyle characterized by simplicity and generosity.

These Moravians were not paid, professionally trained clergy; rather they were laymen and women who wanted to live for Jesus. Leonard Dober and David Zeisberger were two of the missionaries who embodied the spirit of the Moravians. Leonard Dober, a potter by trade, went to the Caribbean island of St. Thomas, where he served among slaves and the native population. For many years, Europeans had colonized St. Thomas but had never taught the slaves about Christ. The Moravians were incensed when they heard testimony of slaves who had no knowledge of Christ. You can imagine the challenges the missionaries faced with just getting to the Caribbean, let alone the dangers of working with the prized possessions of "Christian" slave owners.

Zeisberger immigrated to the New World in 1738 and worked to establish Moravian communities in Georgia and later in New York and Ohio. In 1749 he began to work with Native Americans, a group who by that time were being marginalized. He saw many among the Mohawk, Iroquois, and Algonquian come to faith. He learned their languages and produced dictionaries and religious writings for them to read. British authorities imprisoned him because of his friendship with the native peoples. If not for the Moravian's willingness to put faith in action and to live among the marginalized, both in their home country and other parts of the world, the gospel would not have made it into the lives, families, and cultures of so many.[8]

In 1986, Pam and I led a group of students on a service trip to Haiti. While we were there we met an amazing woman, a Salvation Army captain, Rosmarie Haefeli, known locally as "the angel of San Martin," who worked among the poorest of the poor. The San Martin slum is one of the largest areas of dire poverty in Haiti. That day, as our group went to serve and meet the people of this part of Port au Prince, we were led by this middle-aged, white single woman who had given her life to serve there. She had come to Haiti, from her home in Switzerland, to serve as a nurse. As we walked among the huts and lean-tos, the smell of human waste filled the air and clouds of flies were everywhere. This hunger-ridden community had little reason to have hope, yet whenever the "white angel" appeared there were smiles and waves in return. She spent her days feeding the hungry, caring for the sick, and bringing hope to her people. I remember her face as if it were yesterday.

Rosmarie never became known much outside of her home in San Martin. Her goal was not to be known or famous. This is fitting, as most of us will not become well known, nor will our names show up in a newspaper for the works we do in Jesus' name. And in fact, that is the way it is meant to be. The body of Christ is meant to be a multitude of Christlike ones living out our faith wherever we go. Henri Nouwen puts it this way:

> *Indeed, to live a spiritual life means to become living Christs.*
> *It is not enough to try to imitate Christ as much as possible; it*
> *is not enough to remind others of Jesus; it is not even enough to*
> *be inspired by the words and actions of Jesus Christ. No, the*
> *spiritual life presents us with a far more radical demand: to be*
> *living Christs here and now, in time and history.[9]*

The prophet Ezekiel foresaw a time when God's people would be a restorative influence in the cities of the world. He prophesied,

> *This is what the Sovereign* LORD *says: Once again I will yield*
> *to the plea of the house of Israel and do this for them: I will*
> *make their people as numerous as sheep, as numerous as the*
> *flocks for offerings at Jerusalem during her appointed feasts.*
> *So will the ruined cities be filled with flocks of people. Then*
> *they will know that I am the* LORD. (36:37-38)

I pray that through our lives God will raise up hundreds of thousands of people who are loving and following Jesus, and who are being transformed into men and women who are reflecting the faith, hope, and love seen in Him. May many thousands of us, personal revolutionaries, send out ripples of God's grace across the planet and on into eternity.

QUESTIONS FOR REFLECTION

- Why do you think the statistics show that many professing Christians live lives that are not much different from those who don't profess Christ?
- Is there an area of your life where you could live your faith in a way that would change the world around you? How could you actively live out that truth in a practical way this next week?

PART 5

ETERNAL RIPPLES

Where We Join God's Mission of Grace

CHAPTER 21

MOTIVATION FOR GOD'S MISSION

We implore you on Christ's behalf: Be reconciled to God.

— PAUL (2 CORINTHIANS 5:20)

AS I THINK we've established by now, I love fishing. And I especially love fishing in my float tube—think big truck inner tube with a seat in it! Some of my best days are sitting in that tube, paddling around a high country lake in search of rainbow trout. There's nothing quite like that experience on a calm, cloudless morning, watching the sun begin to reflect off the Collegiate Peaks in South Park in central Colorado. Sitting there waiting for a hefty "bow" to strike, I've learned to listen and watch for the subtle splash and outworking ripples that signal that fish are feeding—the waterborne transmission of good news! I see those ripples and I begin to paddle toward them, even as I wave and shout to let my fishing buddy know the news. The bite is on!

In a similar way, when I came to faith in Christ and began to fully understand the good news and the amazing grace of God, I simply could not keep it to myself. I told the story of what God had done for me to my family and any friends who would listen. Over that first Christmas break during my freshman year of college, I came home and spent time with my friend Brad, who lived across the street. We played tons of ping-pong in the basement of my house and all the while we talked about life. What a thrill it was to tell him about what God had done in mine! He was hungry and interested in hearing more. We spent many hours talking about Jesus.

When we see those ripples of the grace of God in our lives, and we understand their implications for everyone around us, we simply cannot keep the news to ourselves. We must learn how to speak and live the good news of Christ; we must demonstrate the grace of God in the middle of where we live, work, study, and play. In doing this we join a community of other Christ followers who are joining God's mission of grace. We can be part of what God is doing today just as Paul described its impact in the first century: "All over the world this gospel is bearing fruit and growing, just as it has been doing among you since the day you heard it and understood God's grace in all its truth" (Colossians 1:6).

TO THE VERY END OF THE AGE

What compels us to share Christ? What's the heart behind it? Maybe you have heard a sermon, a talk, or even attended a seminar of some sort on how to share your faith or be involved in evangelism. In recent years, Pam and I have interacted with many men and women who desire to see God use them in the lives of people who have yet to experience Jesus. Many tell us they feel unequipped and discouraged in their attempts to be used by God in the advancement of the gospel. Perhaps the evangelism methods they've been taught either don't fit their particular situation, or somehow seem like a sales pitch. Most of us come to realize at some point that these evangelistic tools *alone* are inadequate and at times inappropriate; they can have a similar effect to cutting someone's hair with a gas-powered lawn trimmer. Many of us long to communicate in effective and winsome ways this gospel that is the heart of our existence. We long for the fragrance of the kingdom to waft into the lives of those we know and love, but we sometimes go about it in the wrong way or for the wrong reasons.

During our kids' growing up years, it was standard business in our home for each of us in the family to have weekly chores. Will, our son, is the youngest of the three and the only boy. It sure seemed that the girls, Beth Ann and Lauren, were pretty quick to play the "I'm a girl, that's a boy's job" card in response to our chore distribution. Will mowed the grass and picked up after the dog at an earlier age than they had. Dog duty was definitely his least favorite chore. Usually the routine would happen on the weekend. I'd remind Will of the need to get out in the yard to mow before it would become necessary to rent a Kansas combine. Then I'd hear the classic response from the first chapter of the *Kid's Whining Handbook:* "Whyyyyyy, Dad?!" Too often my response was concise and to the point, "Because I said so!" I obviously didn't pick up that line from any motivational speaker. Some of the parental quotes that have been passed down from generation to generation are pretty embarrassing. Who wrote this stuff?

Did my response fan the flame of Will's passion to do his job? Of course not. In a similar way, we in the body of Christ sometimes resort to curt commands or guilt-triggering needling in an effort to get people to serve God. I believe there are more winsome ways to motivate others to share their faith than the imperative, classic, "because God says so." Instead we can engage others graciously as we embrace God's invitation to share His love and mercy with all. The Great Commission in Matthew 28:18-20 is foundational for our understanding of God's desire for followers of Christ to join Him in His purposes for rescuing the world:

> *All authority in heaven and on earth has been given to me. Therefore go and make disciples of all nations, baptizing them in the name of the Father and of the Son and of the Holy Spirit, and teaching them to obey everything I have commanded you. And surely I am with you always, to the very end of the age.*

This is one of the final statements of Jesus when He walked the earth. It tells us much about God's heart for involvement with Him. God's assignment for us is to make disciples—people who are learners and followers of Jesus. And while it is true that a desire to obey God is a right motivation, there *is* a more complete and compelling motivation for our efforts to bring the good news of Jesus to others. Our involvement as carriers of the good news goes beyond something we *do*. It begins with something we *are*! *It begins with our identity as followers of Jesus*. Where do we learn our primary motivations regarding God's purposes? We look at Jesus Christ. Just as Jesus looked to his Father and lived his life by echoing the words of the Father and embodying the works of the Father, our most compelling motivation comes from following in the steps of Jesus.

SENT AS JESUS WAS SENT

A theme throughout this book has been that at the beginning of time, humanity was created to reflect the character and image of God. One feature of being created in God's image is that in some sense God intends for us to be mirrors that reflect His character before a watching world. After sin entered the world (see Genesis 3), God set in motion a plan to restore us and enable us to once again reflect His image, the image of Jesus Christ (see Romans 8:29; 2 Corinthians 3:18). We have talked in-depth about the transforming work of the gospel and the work of the Holy Spirit, the power that enables this redemptive restoration to occur.

And as we saw in chapter 13, God is a God of mission. The Father, Son, and Holy Spirit exist together as one God who fulfills His redemptive, reconciling, and restoring work in our world. We talked of the perplexing notion that God Himself is *sent*. Jesus Christ, God in human flesh, was *sent* to do the works and will of His Father. One of the deeper and more profound motivations behind our involvement in the Great Commission comes from our identity as *sent ones*.

Bringing the good news of Jesus to a desperate world is not something we have to *do*, it is a natural expression of who we *are*. Shortly after He was raised from the dead, Jesus said to a gathering of His disciples, "Peace be with you! As the Father has sent me, I am sending you" (John 20:21). Just as Jesus' identity was *sent one*, so is ours. Not only are we beloved children of our heavenly Father, but we are also people who are *sent*.

This truth has deeply impacted the way I think about evangelism and the spread of the good news of Christ. *Evangelism* is defined as the proclamation of the message of the good news of Christ. In fact, the spread of the gospel and evangelism have become misunderstood, to the point that many believers see it as something others do, but not something for them! Often we think of evangelism as something that happens at a certain place, at a certain time, using a prescribed method. For many it has come to mean a confronting and uncomfortable activity we can put into our planner. However, there is more to the spread of the gospel than proclaiming the message.

Because my identity as defined by Jesus is *sent one*, every day of the week and every hour of the day, no matter where I am or who I am with, I have the privilege to represent Jesus Christ and to share His good news through word and deed. The apostle Paul, in one of his letters to the Corinthian church, described our role as ambassadors: "We are therefore Christ's ambassadors, as though God were making his appeal through us. We implore you on Christ's behalf: Be reconciled to God" (2 Corinthians 5:20).

The greatest motivation for me, in regard to joining God in His mission is that I have the privilege to be like Jesus: a *sent one*, a courageous ambassador to planet earth.

LOVE AS JESUS LOVED

Not only are we motivated because of how God views us—our identity as *sent ones*—but we are also motivated by the same things that propelled Jesus' life and actions. During the Last Supper, Jesus allowed His followers to see deep within His heart and understand some of His motivations. He knew His time on earth was coming to a close. He said to them, "As the Father has loved me, so have I loved you. Now remain in my love. . . . My command is this: Love each other as I have loved you" (John 15:9,12). Jesus' identity as *sent one* was fueled by love (see John 13:1,31-35; 15:12-13), and so is ours. Later in John's life, he helped the early church understand the kind of love God displayed in His mission to our world,

> Dear friends, let us love one another, for love comes from God. Everyone who loves has been born of God and knows God. Whoever does not love does not know God, because God is love. This is how God showed his love among us: He sent his one and only Son into the world that we might live through him. This is love: not that we loved God, but that he loved us and sent his Son as an atoning sacrifice for our sins. (1 John 4:7-10)

God is the source of love and God's kind of love is a sacrificial, world-engaging love.

A strong motivational foundation for our involvement in God's mission is a desire to love people to Jesus. God spoke through the prophet Jeremiah describing what woos people to God, "The LORD appeared to us in the past, saying: 'I have loved you with an everlasting love; I have drawn you with loving-kindness'" (Jeremiah 31:3).

Jesus described the influence that His followers would have in the world as *light*. He called them "the light of the world" (Matthew 5:14). That passage goes on to say, "In the same way, let your light shine before men, that they may see your good deeds and praise your Father in heaven" (5:16). One of the most natural and powerful ways for the good news of God to advance and for Him to become more famous in the lives of our friends is through acts of love and service.

A number of years ago, we worked to start some communities of twentysomethings in different cities around the country. One of the groups had a great story of the power of love and serving. Some believing friends who lived near a university became acquainted with a student named Abidah and with her Muslim family. Over a period of time, they became friends. Abidah enjoyed hanging out with Andy, Elisabeth, and Joan, whom she came to recognize as people who loved Jesus and had a true connection with God. When Abidah graduated with her degree from the university, her friends Andy, Elisabeth, and Joan were there in the stands, yelling and cheering, holding up signs with Abidah's name and congratulating her on a job well done. None of her other friends were making fools of themselves out of their love for Abidah, and later the three believing friends found that they were the only friends who were invited to the big family party after the ceremony. Abidah was going to be moving away to work on an advanced degree. Her mother told those three believing friends that her daughter didn't realize how much she would be missing them, because they had been such good friends to her.

On an earlier occasion, Abidah had found out that her boyfriend, Nasib, who lived in Afghanistan, was in life-threatening danger. Abidah came straight to Andy and Elisabeth to ask them to pray for Nasib because she knew that they were connected to God, and that, as she said, "their relationship with God was much better than hers." An entire family was exposed to the power of the kingdom through these three friends' acts of love and service. Sacrificial serving love is one of the most genuine motivators for joining God in making waves in our world. And when we live that way, we embody the spirit of Jesus among our friends and family.

COMPASSIONATE LIKE JESUS

Another motivation that reflects the motivation of Jesus is compassion. In Luke 19 we see the heart of Christ in His tears. He is about

234 ~ Making Waves

to enter the city of Jerusalem, just before His crucifixion. He knows that His time is short, and that many there would be accomplices to His murder. "As he approached Jerusalem and saw the city, he wept over it and said, 'If you, even you, had only known on this day what would bring you peace—but now it is hidden from your eyes'" (Luke 19:41-42).

Jesus cared for those who were far from Him. His many hours with the sick, greedy, poor, empty, and demon-possessed were motivated by a heart of compassion. My friend Don Bartel puts it well when he reminds us of the primacy of love and compassion as the starting point for our involvement with not-yet-believing friends:

The second greatest commandment tells us to love our neighbor—the person who lives next door, the person in the next cubicle, the person in an adjacent social network, a brother, sister, cousin . . . these people have needs. If we fail to see their needs, we will likely fail to have compassion for them and to reach out to touch them by meeting their needs.[1]

Over the years, compassionate acts of service have provided an opportunity for friendship and spiritual dialogue with neighbors. Paula and John had a son who was about to begin applying to colleges. They were overwhelmed with sorting through all the information and applications having to do with financial aid and looking for scholarships. Our hearts went out to them in their confusion and fears of that complicated process. We had been there! During a neighborhood get-together we hosted, we got into a discussion about paying for college. Because we had just gone through the same process with one of our kids, I had more current information about the topic than I ever wanted! John and I got together another time to talk and I lent him a book on the topic that helped him sort through what he needed to do in a timeline. He and Paula appreciated all the help, and their anxiety level dropped over those couple of weeks as the road forward began to seem more manageable.

It wasn't very long after our college financing discussions that Pam joined Paula at the gym for a workout. Our friendship had grown to a place of increased trust. During their hour and a half workout, Paula poured out her heart to Pam concerning challenges they were facing with their daughter, Christy. Over a period of weeks, during workouts and over coffee, Pam provided a listening ear, shared challenges she had faced with our girls, and gave Paula some hope. She also had the chance to pray with Paula for her family and ours. One small step at a time, through Pam's life, Paula was being led toward trusting Christ. They later began to read the Bible together.

WHO WE ARE

What does this all mean? The Great Commission — our efforts to advance the gospel and make disciples — is not just something that we *do*. It is who God has designed us to be. We should not try to relegate our involvement in the advance of the gospel to a day or night each week, a training class, or some set of actions that we do, any more than we would separate ourselves from our gender, personality, or fingerprints! *Sentness* is in our DNA; it is who God has created us to *be*. And love and compassion are the motivational forces that inspired Jesus to action.

Therefore, every minute of the day, no matter where I go or what I do, I have the opportunity to reflect the good news of the kingdom. The fragrance of my mission is the same as that of Jesus: the love that the Father has for me. The aroma of my outreach is the same compassion that brought tears to the eyes of Jesus. In a wonderful promise, God declares it is His job to make this happen in our lives: "But thanks be to God, who always leads us in triumphal procession in Christ and through us spreads everywhere the fragrance of the knowledge of him" (2 Corinthians 2:14).

QUESTIONS FOR REFLECTION

- When you think about sharing your faith with others, what tends to motivate you and what tends to hinder you?
- Read John 20:21 three times. In what ways could you more fully live like a "sent one" this week?

CHAPTER 22

BRINGING *ALL* THE GOOD NEWS OF JESUS TO THE WORLD

For God so loved the world that he gave his one and only Son, that whoever believes in him shall not perish but have eternal life.

— JESUS (JOHN 3:16)

OUR VIEW OF the good news of Jesus and the kingdom greatly influences our values and the methods we choose in our efforts to advance the gospel.

Historically, members of the body of Christ have tended to live out their faith with an emphasis on one or the other of two understandings of the gospel message. Some believers focus on the present power of the good news and the kingdom represented by the gospel's current impact in people's lives and the socially transforming aspects of the gospel. Other parts of the church focus on the future power of the good news that is seen in the redemptive work of the Cross and the eternal hope the gospel brings for people as individuals. There is a danger of distorting the gospel and its effects at either end of the spectrum.

If we only see the good news embodied in present-day expressions of the kingdom, our attempts to spread the good news may be limited to acts of love and service. If we consider the good news only a list of steps to eternal life, our efforts will be limited to content-oriented presentations that are only deemed successful when people give assent to those truths. The good news of Jesus has broader effects than entrance to heaven; it has grand implications both for today and for eternity.

I believe that biblical truth includes both of these aspects of the gospel. Consider these biblical ideas that capture the essence and effect of the good news of Jesus:

- captives freed
- sin forgiven
- broken hearts mended
- reconciliation
- prisoners released
- regeneration
- blind healed
- redemption
- yokes lifted
- justification
- hungry fed
- thirst quenched
- abundant life
- eternal life
- adoption
- peace
- restoration
- Christ in you
- lame walking
- transformation

Clearly, some of these speak to the present power of the good news in the lives of people and the society they inhabit. Others reflect the future hope we have of a restored, eternal relationship with God.

THROUGH DEED AND THROUGH WORD

As Jesus began His ministry in Galilee, the message He proclaimed was the good news of the kingdom of God, "After John was put in prison, Jesus went into Galilee, proclaiming the good news of God. 'The time has come,' he said. 'The kingdom of God is near. Repent and believe the good news!'" (Mark 1:14-15).

This good news demanded a decision. He was calling them to turn from one set of allegiances and to believe the good news associated with the reign of God. Would they turn from their current dependencies and embrace the good news that the God-King was offering? Allegiance to the rule of this new king would bring a dramatic change of life and a new set of kingdom-of-light values.

Throughout Jesus' ministry our Savior proclaims and demonstrates the good news of the kingdom. Usually, we think of "good news" in terms of what Jesus said and the message associated with His death on the cross. But consider, if you will, what you would find if you were to read the gospel of Mark, and make a list of all the ways that people experienced the good news because Jesus Christ brought the power of the kingdom into our world? Your list might include:

- demons overpowered
- children loved
- hungry people fed
- leprosy healed
- children healed
- fishermen rescued
- broken lives mended
- sins paid for

These are all ways people experienced good news through what Jesus *did*!

Every four years we see a bunch of politicians announcing their bid for the White House. Pretty quickly they showcase their special message: the drumbeat of values that will set them apart from the rest of the pack. Though He had no interest in political office, Jesus did make an announcement early in His ministry at a synagogue in His boyhood home of Nazareth. His message was the message of the kingdom, taken from the mouth of the prophet Isaiah: "The Spirit of the Lord is on me, because he has anointed me to preach good news to the poor. He has sent me to proclaim freedom for the prisoners and recovery of sight for the blind, to release the oppressed, to proclaim the year of the Lord's favor" (Luke 4:18-19).

Clearly Jesus' method for sharing the good news included words, but it also included actions that led to immediate deliverance for His followers. Because our view of the good news has a huge effect on how we share it with our family and friends, it is important that we understand the good news in a way that honors what God has revealed in the Scriptures. To this end, consider the following three illustrations that help us to see different aspects of the good news that God intends for us to experience and, in turn, for others to experience through us.

THE BRIDGE TO THE CASTLE

First, picture the bridge over a moat surrounding a great and majestic castle. The bridge provides the way to the door of the castle and invites us to the home of the King. The bridge over the water represents God's various interventions in our lives and others that He has used to propel us along the path toward Him.

Personally, God revealed Himself to me by bringing good news at key points in my life before I began to follow Christ. I told of the time God answered the prayer of a young second baseman who believed God could help his Little League team win over the reigning champs.

Another kingdom-sighting was the time God calmed my heart and brought hope when I was sixteen years old and was lonely and depressed after moving and changing schools for the second time in three years. God connected me with a God-fearing football coach who invited me to Fellowship of Christian Athlete meetings. It was there that I connected with some new friends and first heard passages from the Bible applied to everyday life. A couple of years later, it was the influence of Christ-following friends in college who loved me and showed me Jesus. They were evidence of the good news of God for my life. While I was on the bridge moving toward Christ, the kind actions of friends led me forward.

Early in His ministry, Jesus had just come back from a ministry trip to the east side of the Sea of Galilee. The gospel writer Mark tells us that a synagogue ruler named Jairus came to Him and begged Jesus to come with him to his home because his young daughter was dying. As Jesus, Jairus, and some of the disciples made their way to the synagogue ruler's home, they stopped along the way to tend to a sick woman. While en route to the house, news came to them that the little girl had died. Jesus said to Jairus, "Don't be afraid; just believe" (Mark 5:36).

In the end, Jesus raised the little girl from the dead. The influence of this miracle is not limited to Jairus and his daughter, of course; it has a profound impact on all the family members. Mark preserved the intimacy of the moment by retaining the caring Aramaic phrase Jesus uttered, "*Talitha koum!*" The Aramaic translation is, "Little girl, I say to you, get up!" (Mark 5:41). Now we don't know what happened to Jairus. Did he begin to follow Jesus? We really don't know. We can assume, however, that the little girl, her father and all the family were touched deeply and each one moved along the path and "bridge" toward the doorway of decision, through the loving deeds of Jesus.

Through history, some have called this kind of good news common grace—the goodness of God experienced by both those who ultimately come into the kingdom and those who do not. This first portrait—the bridge—is seen in the kingdom work of Jesus as He related to, served, and loved everyday broken people, patiently displaying the heart of a loving, forgiving, powerful God-King among those who did not yet believe in Him. It is this incremental work of God, usually through His people, that leads people toward Jesus. It may happen when a meal is brought to a sick neighbor, a visit is made to an elderly man in a nursing home, or when a kind word is spoken to a barista who has had a hard day. The good news of Jesus and the kingdom is seen in deeds that embody the heart of King Jesus in our world.

THE DOORWAY OF THE CASTLE

Our second portrait of kingdom good news is the doorway to the castle. Consider a large, red castle door. It is the entryway into the home of a loving, majestic, and all-powerful King. The door represents the message of the atonement, reconciliation, and redemption. The door promises new birth and entry into the full effects of the gospel. Here we consider key gospel passages such as 1 Corinthians 15, 2 Corinthians 5:21, and Romans 3:21-26.

Jesus put it this way: "For God so loved the world that he gave his one and only Son, that whoever believes in him shall not perish but have eternal life" (John 3:16).

The Scriptures attest to the salvation that is found in Jesus. Consider these people who came to the doorway of the castle and entered into salvation, eternal life, and relationship with God through the message of grace:

- Peter (see John 6:68)
- Zacchaeus (see Luke 19:9)
- The criminal crucified next to Jesus (see Luke 23:41-43)
- The Ethiopian official (see Acts 8:35-37)
- Lydia, the Philippian business woman (see Acts 16:14-15)
- The Philippian jailer (see Acts 16:29-33)

And through the expanding story in the book of Acts, we see that the ripple effect of God's saving grace, beginning in Jerusalem, was continuing to reverberate powerfully (see Acts 2:47; Colossians 1:6).

Apart from faith and the work of Jesus Christ on the cross, there is no doorway into the kingdom of God. Each person makes entrance to the goodness of God's kingdom when he or she responds to the good news of the redemptive work of Jesus Christ.

THE BANQUET HALL

The final portrait illustrating the good news of Jesus and the kingdom is the banquet hall. Picture the great banquet hall in a castle, bursting with an unrestrained, joy-filled party. Imagine the high stone walls and an immense great room filled with warmth from many fireplaces. There is dancing, food and drink, laughter, friendship, and the interaction of family and friends who have experienced healing and are continuing to encounter restoration at the hand of the King and His people.

The picture of the banquet hall represents good news for followers of Jesus. He no longer sees us as sinners or slaves, but as His children and heirs of all He possesses. Here are some examples of this good news for those who are in Christ:

- Adoption as sons and daughters (see Romans 8:13-17; Galatians 4:4-7)
- Transformation (see 2 Corinthians 3:17-18)
- Holy Spirit (see John 14:16-17; Galatians 5:16-26; Titus 3:5-7)
- Peace and hope (see Romans 5:1-5; Colossians 1:21-27)
- Freedom and release from captivity (see Matthew 11:28-30; Luke 4:18-19; Galatians 5:1)

The good news of Jesus is not something that just gets us through the door; it is freeing and restoring for every Christ follower every day.

As sons and daughters of the King, we enjoy peace and freedom from guilt and shame because of what Jesus Christ has done. Remember, how we view the gospel impacts how—or even if—we will share our faith. When you consider the good news of the kingdom as expressed in these three ways, it opens up a host of opportunities and ways that we can be ambassadors of the good news through our lives, our actions, and our words. While ushering people through the door and helping them understand and experience new birth are central and important, there are vast opportunities for all of us to engage with not-yet-believing people on their way to the kingdom—to allow them to see an expression of kingdom love or service through our lives. And there are opportunities for us to help fellow Christ followers join the "party," coming into greater participation and experience of the good news of Jesus in their everyday lives.

QUESTIONS FOR REFLECTION

- Do you feel more comfortable sharing your faith through words or through actions? What hinders you in the other? What is one small step you could take this next week to share your faith in a new way?
- Review the three illustrations of the good news in this chapter. Before you began following Christ, in what ways did you experience the good news that ultimately led you toward Jesus?
- Think back to the banquet hall illustration. Which of these do you desire to experience more fully: adoption, transformation, the work of the Holy Spirit, peace, hope, or freedom? Ask God to help you experience these aspects of the good news.

CHAPTER 23

THE FOURTEEN-FOOT WALL

The Word became flesh and blood, and moved into the neighborhood.

— JOHN (JOHN 1:14, MSG)

OVER THE YEARS we have worked closely with students, both in our local church and through ministries such as The Navigators and Young Life. One summer we did a team-building activity with a group of college students at a ropes course at Eagle Lake Camp in the mountains outside Colorado Springs. Part of the course was the fourteen-foot wall. The goal was to have everyone on the team get over it quickly. To say we struggled on that obstacle is an understatement. We ended up dropping two team members on top of each other from the top of the wall! We finally asked for help.

What is the fourteen-foot wall in our efforts to bring the good news of Christ to a world needing hope? It is the challenge of developing meaningful friendships with those who need Jesus. It is here that we often get stymied in our gospel advancing efforts. People who are feeling stalled in their efforts to reach those yet to know Jesus Christ need only employ a few simple strategies.

During early 2007 I helped organize a group of about one

hundred men and women from around the country in a project to learn how the good news of Jesus and His kingdom spreads among friends and through social networks. These men and women, most of them in their twenties and early thirties, were part of fifteen small community groups in eight cities. We spent a year learning together and actively loving and engaging people in our normal spheres of life. Some common statements and questions posed by participants during that learning experience were:

- "We know we need to meet and know more people who don't know Christ."
- "What do we do between the time we meet them and the time they are ready to embrace Christ?"

From our interactions in that learning community, we discerned two major barriers that stand in the way of our bringing people to Jesus Christ:

1. Many believers have few natural interactions (outside of work) with people yet to know Christ.
2. While many Christ followers know people who are not yet following Jesus, they have not chosen to develop meaningful friendships with them.

OUT OF THE BUBBLE

Many call it the "bubble." It's where followers of Christ can find themselves living, without even realizing it. Cloistered in a Christian subculture, life gets busy and you find yourself with little time to give to any relationships, let alone to friendships with people yet to embrace Jesus. Work, family, church, and if we can find time, leisure activities can fill our schedules to overflowing.

Many years ago, I was attending seminary and working as an

apartment manager. I was spending a lot of time studying, and I was involved in church activities. A pastor friend, who worked with men in the community, invited me to go out to lunch with a group of men, some of whom were not yet followers of Christ. We met at a historic pizza place called Bonnie Brae Tavern. I remember it like it was yesterday. It was a fun, outgoing group of men. Those who were followers of Christ mixed easily with those who were not yet believers, some pretty rough around the edges. I watched those believers engage in conversation with their friends about the things that mattered to them. They talked about fast cars, sports, finances, and their work. As I sat there, a disturbing thought erupted in my mind—"I have absolutely nothing to add to this conversation." Being immersed in Scripture and hanging out with other believers in a seminary setting had brought me to the point of having little to add to a dialogue with the very people I longed to help.

Many Christians are no more conversant in life than I was. Have you ever heard the phrase, "So heavenly minded, of no earthly good?" That was me. It was a humbling lesson. Maybe you have found yourself in a similar situation: A full life, with many activities squeezing out friendships with people in need of Jesus? Let me provide a few strategies that may help you get out of the bubble.

FINDING THIRD PLACES

If having no natural interactions (outside of work) with people yet to know Christ is a major barrier for believers, finding a "third place" is one step on the journey over that barrier. Isolation from a broken world was not an option for Jesus, and it should not be for those of us seeking to live as sent ones.

I love the way Jesus (the Word) is described in the first chapter of John's gospel in *The Message*: "The Word became flesh and blood, and moved into the neighborhood" (1:14). Jesus came from heaven to earth to move into our neighborhood. Now we need to make the effort to do the same—to engage with the people God has placed right outside our front door and in the normal pathways of our lives.

Some businesses and marketing executives have recently coined the term "third place." It is a helpful idea for those of us wanting to get out of the bubble. In fact, a few years ago, in a conversation with a manager friend at Starbucks, I discovered that Starbucks works to be *the* third place for people, close to where they live. The first place is our home. The second place is where we work. The third place is where we spend our spare time. Some sociologists believe that the third place is where people are most open to friendships and connecting with others. Do you want to get to know some people who are not yet walking with Christ? A good place to start would be to become a participant or a regular in a third place.

Pam and I have intentionally limited and changed our traffic patterns over the past decade. Rather than frequenting five different coffee shops, three grocery stores, seven different restaurants, and three workout venues, we've brought focus to where we hang out. It started with our interactions at the YMCA and at Liberty High School sports activities during our kids' high school years. Right there in our normal traffic patterns were friendships waiting to happen: regulars at the Y and parents and families involved with the soccer team. Our lives are so much richer because of the friendships developed at Liberty sporting events! We then adopted a local coffee shop as our hangout spot. Most days we stop by to sit, read, and see the regulars and people who work there. I am there right now, writing these words, sipping on a tea. For a few years, we decided to show up at a local Mexican restaurant every week or two. The managers and wait-staff got to know us and call us by name. We got to know more about them and to connect with them about their families, dreams, and life challenges.

Earlier, I mentioned the fifteen groups that were started around the country. These groups tried out various ways to connect with their not-yet-believing acquaintances in the hopes that friendships would develop. Here are some of the "third places" they frequented or developed. A group in Seattle started a gaming night and invited friends to play video games every week on the same night. Another Seattle group adopted a local coffee shop and even began to show up at the same time each week, finding some of the same people there every week. A group in Minneapolis joined friends at the karaoke night at a local pub. A Denver group went with friends to a concert in Boulder, and when they invited coworkers and members of their community to a house-warming party, seventy people showed up. A couple of moms in Lansing joined together with other moms for a weekly playgroup. The time together allowed them to get to know one another and establish deeper connections around family issues. The husbands of these moms joined a basketball league and a softball league, where they met other men in their community.

In years past, Pam and I have hosted going-away parties for manager friends from our coffee shop. Those parties helped us become better friends with the employees and regulars from the store. Being in our home moved some of the friendships to a new level. During one of my visits to our local coffee shop, a friend of our son came running up to me and said, "Mr. Nuenke, I'm interested in finding out about Jesus and heard you could help!"

We had known Greg for about four years. He had played on a soccer team with Will before high school. Greg's dad, Larry, had been one of the coaches of that team, so we had many opportunities to relate to them and their family during games and team parties. They were from a Jewish background and Greg had gone through his Bar Mitzvah a year earlier. During high school, Greg continued to be friends with Will and several other Christ-following students. Through their lives and words, Greg had been drawn closer and closer to Christ.

At that time, Greg was going through a very challenging season. There were family issues that were weighing heavily on him. I told Greg that I'd love to get together with him. A week later, our son Will and I talked with Greg over coffee and tea. More than anything, Greg really needed a listening ear to allow him to share some of what was going on in his family and how it was impacting him. Will and I also answered some of his questions regarding Christ, but he wasn't ready to make a decision. That encounter was a new installment of good news for Greg, adding to what God had been doing for some time in his heart. If not for our commitment to living among those yet to know Christ and inhabiting "third places" like the soccer sideline and our local coffee shop, that important encounter would never have happened. We'll continue the story of God's work in Greg's life in a later chapter.

The first secret is this: We must resist the temptation to huddle and instead choose to live among those yet to know Christ. One application is through engaging in a "third place" or developing one. Have you moved into your "neighborhood" or are you living in the safety of the fringes? May God give us the courage, love, compassion, and servant-spirit to join Jesus in the middle of our world that is without hope and without God. You can only make waves if you are in the pool!

GETTING ON THE TOP-FIVE LIST

Another issue we face is that many of us have not developed friend-ships of depth with others yet to know Christ. The gospel flows most naturally through genuine friendships.

Ten years ago, Pam and I began asking ourselves if we were on the "top five list" of any people that did not yet know Christ. Were there any not-yet-believing people who would consider us among the first they would call in a time of crisis? We were dismayed to realize that, beyond a few extended family members, we could think of none who counted us as close friends. We wondered how it happened that while pursuing Christian ministry full-time, we'd come to live life in a "holy huddle." Our lives together hadn't begun that way. We began to ask God to teach us and give us opportunity to break out of that rut. We asked God to help us have friendships with not-yet-believing people. It has been exciting to see God answer those prayers.

We are all acquainted with people who are not following Christ.

And some of us know how to share an illustration like the "Bridge Illustration" or the "Four Spiritual Laws" with someone who is ready to "make a decision" and come to faith in Christ. Yet without real friendships, we will have no recourse but to limit our efforts to premature gospel presentations and inviting people we hardly know to events. Outside of inviting not-yet-believing people to church, what is the answer?

In the Sermon on the Mount in Matthew 5–7, Jesus colorfully describes what life in His kingdom is meant to look like. He starts with the Beatitudes, which reflect a kind of profile for followers of Christ. Right after the foundation of the Beatitudes, God directs our attention to the kind of influence kingdom citizens are meant to have in the world: "You are the salt of the earth. . . . You are the light of the world" (Matthew 5:13-14).

Salt is a preservative and light is a vanquisher of darkness. Both permeate the environments they are meant to influence. This so aptly describes the influence God intends for us as we live among those without the hope of the gospel. The powerful gospel of Jesus is best experienced up close and personal. As we move intentionally to develop meaningful friendships with those yet to know Christ, they will get close enough to see, experience, and hear the good news of Jesus.

While there *are* those Spirit-inspired circumstances such as when Philip met an Ethiopian man reading the Scripture and hungering for an explanation, most folks are not ready for a whole package explanation of faith during our first conversation. We need to learn a whole new skill set—to enjoy and participate patiently in redemptive friendships with those yet to embrace Jesus.

THERE IS HOPE

Our identity as *sent ones* demands that we learn these lessons, and a world filled with downcast and discouraged people cries out for us to courageously apply them. Know that there is hope. You can develop

252 ~ Making Waves

redemptive friendships, but it will demand a change in thinking and small changes in the way you live.

If we want to be used by God to bring the good news of Christ to our world, we must become convinced of the need to enter into their world. Otherwise we will relegate ourselves outside the world of those we long to reach and rescue.

Many followers of Jesus want to have their friends experience the good news of the kingdom and say that they want to learn how to have authentic, fun, lasting, and intentional friendships with people who have not yet found Christ. In the chapters that follow, we'll look at more ideas for how to help our not-yet-believing friends and family move toward Christ.

QUESTIONS FOR REFLECTION

- What do you think keeps many Christ followers from having meaningful relationships with people yet to know Jesus?
- Is there a "third place" where you could begin to spend time, with the hope of making friends with people in need of the gospel?
- Write down the names of one or two non-believing people with whom you would like to develop a deeper friendship. Pray for God's help and insights into those friendships.

CHAPTER 24

REDEFINING EVANGELISM

I hope that every encounter I have with a person will work toward leading them closer to Christ.

— GARY BRADLEY

A NUMBER OF years ago, I met a man named Scott while working out at the gym. Though I'm not a workout fanatic, I go often enough to recognize the regulars. Scott had helped coach a baseball team in a league both our sons belonged to. I had seen him on the baseball field, so I recognized him when I saw him at the club. It wasn't long before we were talking about our sons' involvement in sports. Over a period of months, we slowly got to know one another better and our conversations gradually expanded to other topics. At one point I found out that I had a friend who worked for Scott's brother. This person was another believer. Over a period of eighteen months, Scott and I had lunch together a few times. We talked about life, our jobs, our families, and his church involvement while growing up.

During one of our lunches, Scott mentioned that his wife was in a Bible study. I asked him if he'd ever be interested in something like that.

"No, I don't know enough," was his reply.

He said that his lack of spiritual knowledge made him fearful to attend anything with people he felt knew more than he did. I told him that I could read the Bible with him periodically if he was interested. I suggested that because we were friends, we didn't need to worry about how much we knew or didn't know. We decided it would be fun to read a bit each week together. We started meeting one morning a week for thirty to forty-five minutes. It was messy. Our schedules didn't always work out. Some months even went by when we couldn't get together. It took us two years to go through the gospel of Luke. During that time, I was also able to show him the Bridge illustration, a tool developed by The Navigators (see appendix B), to investigate the idea of grace and relationship with God.

From the time we began meeting together, it took two years and several months for Scott to begin to understand grace and leave behind his works-oriented view of spirituality. Then, slowly, the light of the gospel began to dawn. One morning Scott got quiet and a bit more serious than usual. He told me that when we first started reading the Bible together he really had little personal desire to do so. He just thought that it might be "good for him." Then Scott paused and he told me that his attitude had changed. He described how he now had a desire to know God and learn more from the Scriptures. He said that he now understands that it is faith in Christ that determines a person's spiritual status, not how many good things he does. With a smile on his face, Scott told me that he wanted to grow spiritually and that he had a desire to help others too.

PARTNERING WITH GOD

I know very few things as exciting as seeing someone come to know Jesus. I'm so glad that over those three years, I never had the inclination to move on to more "fertile soil." While God allowed us to see the fruit of change in Scott's life, we are still waiting to see such change in the lives of other friends we are getting to know.

I would not say that I am a patient person by nature. However, it seems that one of the key principles of the kingdom and in spreading the good news of Christ is that, usually, much patience is required in waiting for the seed of the gospel to sprout. I love the parable Jesus told in Mark 4:26-29:

> This is what the kingdom of God is like. A man scatters seed on the ground. Night and day, whether he sleeps or gets up, the seed sprouts and grows, though he does not know how. All by itself the soil produces grain—first the stalk, then the head, then the full kernel in the head. As soon as the grain is ripe, he puts the sickle to it, because the harvest has come.

This parable points out two sets of responsibility: ours and God's. Our responsibility is to scatter the seed of the gospel of the kingdom through our actions and our words. God's job is the growth of the seed until it reaches maturity. At the appropriate time, it is also our role to harvest the grain. This means that in addition to scattering the seed of the gospel over time, we should also be ready to help people make the final step—to embrace Jesus Christ when they come to the place of ripeness. This is where a tool like the Bridge illustration or the Romans Road can be helpful.

It's interesting that the man in the parable didn't lie awake at night wondering if the seed would sprout. It wouldn't hurry things up for him to get up and peer out the window. Much of helping people come to know Jesus requires similar faith and trust. We must patiently wait for God to bring people to readiness. In 1 Corinthians 3:6-7, Paul speaks of the partnership we have with God: "I planted the seed, Apollos watered it, but God made it grow. So neither he who plants nor he who waters is anything, but only God, who makes things grow."

God gets all the glory, but we have the extraordinary privilege to do our part in sharing the grace of God that also set us free!

RUNNING THE RELAY RACE

During the 2008 Beijing Olympics I watched the track and field relay finals. It was Jeremy Wariner who ran the anchor leg of the event and took the baton across the tape for the U.S. in the 4X400 relay. That performance won the finals and set a new Olympic record, beating out teams from the Bahamas and Russia. The most exciting time in the race was watching Wariner sprint for home. The young athlete was a hero that day; he was the one who crossed the finish line like a lightning bolt. But as important as that anchor leg performance was, when it came time to ascend the winners' platform and receive a gold medal, Wariner was just one runner among a team that included LaShawn Merritt, Angelo Taylor, and David Neville. It took all of those fleet feet to win that race.

If we think about the advancement of the good news of Christ and the influence of the kingdom only in terms of people making a decision to follow Christ, we will be tempted to see success in a very limited way that only celebrates the "anchor leg." We will be tempted to count the number of people coming to faith and to ignore the slower and less obvious work that God is doing in moving people toward faith in Christ. Of course we celebrate and work toward seeing people make the decision to follow Christ. However the groundwork that precedes that decision is equally important. God's hand is evident in each step of the journey to faith, and it is worth our time to be involved in the scattering as well as the reaping. Each of us has a role to play in seeing people move closer to Christ and eventually cross the tape into the kingdom.

As *sent ones*, every encounter we have with another person, believer or not, has purpose. We live intentionally, desiring that our actions and words draw others to Christ, but we must be careful not to develop a distorted agenda that is so focused on winning souls that we treat people differently when they don't please us or follow our plan. Our kingdom purpose as *sent ones* invites us to live redemptively in every season of our relationships.

The stories people tell of how they came to follow Jesus are as unique as fingerprints! I often find myself close to tears as I hear the creative ways God lovingly pursues and wins our attention. And in each step of those journeys there were individuals who played unique roles to prompt, love, and exhort people forward toward Christ. Each of us has a role to play in the lives of others. For some it will be giving a kind word in the name of Christ. For others, it will be acts of service, as small as a meal for someone just home from the hospital or picking up the mail while a neighbor is out of town. In some cases, we will explain the good news of Christ to a person for the first time, a seed that will not sprout till years later. And it really doesn't matter which leg of the race we are running, but that we are in the race.

MOVING THEM ALONG THE PATH

What would it look like if our "evangelism," our living as *sent ones*, was less agenda-driven and rushed, and more characterized by love, patience, authenticity, and confidence that the Spirit knows the right timing? What would it look like to enter into friendships with a long-term perspective? What if we had a commitment to growing friendships regardless of whether or not things went the way we wanted them to go in terms of individuals coming to know Christ?

If you want to make people perspire, all you need to do is ask this question of a group of believers: "When is the last time you led someone to Christ?" Over the years, evangelism training has often focused on "reaping" and a destination mentality versus one of "sowing" and walking alongside another on the pathway to Jesus. Likewise, salvation has been viewed from a point-in-time perspective rather than as the process of coming to faith. What if "leading someone to Christ" was redefined? My friend, Gary Bradley, has said, "I hope that every encounter I have with a person will work toward leading them closer to Christ."

The world is filled with people on a spiritual journey. Many are not yet ready to attend church or a Christian event or to make a decision to follow Christ. However, they may be open to relationships and ready to make small decisions that will move them closer to Christ.

Elle is someone who used to work at a tapas restaurant that Pam and I frequent. We got to know Elle over a period of two years and she eventually became the store's assistant manager. Pam and I both grew to be her friends and tried to love her in tangible ways, through gifts on her birthday and through words of affirmation. When a friend of ours hit it big in the music world, we set up a concert for him to play at the restaurant. The concert was a huge success and filled the place to capacity with fans. Elle sold a lot of food and she was amazed that we had set that up for her. When she was moved to take a new job in Chicago, we hosted a going-away party at our home. Though, as far as we know, she hasn't experienced a new birth in Christ, we are confident that Elle saw Jesus and experienced kingdom good news through our lives. She wrote us this note after the going away party:

> Thank You! Words cannot express what it meant to me that you two opened your home to our restaurant for my going away party. At TerrificTapas, I always hope that I make a difference in someone's day, so thanks for making mine, not just today, but every day that you came in. It has been a pleasure being a part of your lives, and thank you for making me feel like my job is less about work and more about community. Best Wishes! Elle

We are hopeful that by God's grace He used us to help Elle move along the path toward Jesus.

THE HARVEST WILL COME

Remember our soccer friends, Greg and his father, Larry? The year following Greg's initial inquiry at our local coffee shop was pretty exciting, with lots of ups and downs. After a couple of months, Greg showed up at the Bible reading group that my son Will and I hosted at our house for some of his friends. His interest and understanding of Jesus and the gospel grew. Over time, Will and his believing friend Jeff encouraged Greg and answered his questions as they arose. One Sunday afternoon, Will, Jeff, and I met Greg at the coffee shop and summarized the ideas of grace and a relationship with God through the use of the Bridge illustration. Though Greg was not ready to make a decision to follow Christ that day, when asked where he would put himself in relation to God he said, "I'm right here in the middle [of the bridge], but I'm sprinting toward God!" Greg eventually did make a decision to follow Christ and is continuing to grow and develop in his character and ability to lead others. In the midst of it all, Greg's mom, Martha, began to make steps toward Jesus, and I continue to pray for his dad, Larry. This all took place over a period of three years, during which we loved, served, and enjoyed our friendship with that family. Our interactions were consistent, though not frequent. Like the farmer, it is hard to figure out how these seeds have sprouted. It has clearly been something God has done through many people.

My experience, as well as the pattern of Scripture, tells me that through patience, sowing, and befriending, we can all see dozens of people wooed ever closer to the kingdom through the fragrance of Christ they see, feel, smell, and touch in our lives. Along the way, we need to be ready for those who are ready to become kingdom citizens as soon as we meet them. I suspect that in most instances when this occurs, it will happen because other sent ones have already patiently loved and lived out the kingdom in front of these individuals! I believe that if we redefined evangelism to mean leading each person we encounter one step closer to Jesus, we would find many, many more people perspiring less and feeling more excited about committing their personalities, talents, spiritual gifts, and time to advancing the gospel of Jesus and His kingdom. For each of us, the important question is "What leg of the relay am I uniquely prepared to run in this person's life?" And then jump in that race!

QUESTIONS FOR REFLECTION

- Think of someone in your life who is yet-to-know Jesus. Could you patiently begin to trust God to use you in his or her life? Pray that person's eyes would be open to God's goodness and grace.
- What are one or two ways you could begin to live differently that would help everyone you interact with to see Jesus in your life?

CHAPTER 25

LIVES THAT CARRY THE GOSPEL

How beautiful on the mountains are the feet of those who bring good news.

— ISAIAH (ISAIAH 52:7)

MOST OF US are not going to preach to thousands in filled stadiums, and most of us are not persuasive communicators or able to winsomely convince someone of his or her need for Christ in a single sitting. I've been around great preachers and proclaimers of the gospel, and I've known some very gifted people for whom every conversation seems to be a natural on-ramp to a talk about Jesus Christ. What about the rest of us? As we have seen in previous pages, every one of us is sent and given the privilege of representing Jesus and the kingdom in our world. So what are some practical ways that the rest of us (the non-preachers and non-evangelists) can bring the good news of Christ into our everyday worlds?

One of my favorite Old Testament gospel verses is Isaiah 52:7: "How beautiful on the mountains are the feet of those who bring good news, who proclaim peace, who bring good tidings, who proclaim salvation, who say to Zion, 'Your God reigns!'"

Do you have beautiful feet? Certainly, the credibility and power of the message of Christ is affected positively or negatively by the life of the one who speaks the message. As we have discussed, God is in the business of changing us into people who more fully reflect His character. When people see the love and character of Christ in us it provides our not-yet-believing friends living proof that our message is true and allows God to use our lives to draw people to Himself.

SERVING IN CHRIST'S NAME

It was late in the day and I was working hard to get my final paperwork done before shutting the lights off at the office. Then the phone rang. *Should I answer or not? Oh well, why not?* On the other end of the phone was Ruth Ramona, an elderly woman who would become a part of our lives during those years we lived in Lawrence, Kansas.

Several months earlier, a group of us had decided to organize "Project Serve," an effort to mobilize university students at the University of Kansas. Our hope was to serve some of the senior citizens in the community in the name of Jesus. We put up posters, took out ads in the newspaper, and made announcements in local churches. The requests for help came fast and furious! Folks asked us to rake leaves, clean houses, and help with home repairs. Our team of seven recruited college students to assist us and began to schedule opportunities to serve. We met and were able to serve many elderly people in Lawrence, and it opened up many opportunities to represent Jesus.

Ruth Ramona had seen an ad in the paper and was calling to see if she could get someone to drive her to the grocery store sometime later in the week. After checking with Pam, I decided to invite her over for dinner that evening with our family. I was amazed when this woman I had never met accepted my offer. She gave me directions and I went to pick her up. In the years that followed, we helped Ruth in various ways and shared the good news of Jesus with her. In her final years of life, we visited her at her nursing home. Finally, she moved to another part of Kansas to be closer to family and we ended up losing touch. We aren't sure if she ever decided to trust Christ, but there is no doubt that she heard the message and saw the effect of Jesus in our lives. She brought so much into our family during that season. It was nice to have another friend in town, especially one who had stories to tell about growing up as a child on the Kansas plains. Ruth shared with our family her stories from her real-life "Little House on the Prairie!"

The apostle Peter, in his letter to the scattered churches of Asia Minor, wrote this about the effect of a good life, "Live such good lives among the pagans that, though they accuse you of doing wrong, they may see your good deeds and glorify God on the day he visits us" (1 Peter 2:12). Perhaps there is not a better way to obey Peter's command as to simply reach out to serve those in our community. As we live, walk, and befriend those yet to know Jesus Christ, we draw others to Him.

THE POWER OF AFFIRMATION

Many people I talk with bring up how difficult it is for them to bring up spiritual topics in their conversations with non-Christian friends. During the past few years, I have made a personal discovery that has opened my eyes to a new way to connect with people at a deeper level. It's a way to appreciate and encourage people, touching them at a heart level in a way that affirms who God has made them to be.

Earlier, when discussing the topic of faith in chapter 16, we considered the faith of the Roman centurion whose servant was sick (see Matthew 8). Remember, the centurion told Jesus that he didn't even need to come to his house to heal the servant and that he believed Jesus could heal from a distance. We have no indication that this Roman leader was a follower of Christ, but he certainly had some aspect of faith (from Luke 7 we know he had favor with the Jews). Even so, Jesus' words of affirmation for this Roman soldier must have been shocking for the religious leaders who were looking on and life-altering for the soldier, "I tell you the truth, I have not found anyone in Israel with such great faith" (Matthew 8:10). Even in this brief interaction, Jesus had seen the heart of this man, identified something that reflected the heart of God, and affirmed it. I imagine that it must have felt as if Jesus was identifying one of the most precious areas of the soldier's heart and declaring it to be of value.

A sincere affirmation can be a powerful means for engaging people at a heart level, identifying something in them that God values. Though sin has tarnished and twisted God's creation, every person still reflects in various ways the image of God. Romans 1:20 gives testimony to this fact: "For since the creation of the world God's invisible qualities — his eternal power and divine nature — have been clearly seen, being understood from what has been made." All creation — the mountains, flowers, sunsets, powerful tornadoes, the stars, and *man himself*—gives testimony to the divine nature of God. Psalm 8 speaks of the worth of every individual:

O LORD, our Lord,
   how majestic is your name in all the earth!
You have set your glory
   above the heavens.
From the lips of children and infants
   you have ordained praise
because of your enemies,
   to silence the foe and the avenger.

When I consider your heavens,
   the work of your fingers,
the moon and the stars,
   which you have set in place,
what is man that you are mindful of him,
   the son of man that you care for him?
You made him a little lower than the heavenly beings
   and crowned him with glory and honor. (verses 1-5)

Admittedly, it's easier to see God's image in some people than it is in others. However, if we prayerfully ask God to help us to see those around us as He views them, we can begin to see the fingerprints of God in the life of each person we meet.

Let me give you an example of how affirmation works. Several years ago, when I first came upon this principle of affirmation, I was driving with a friend, coming home from a retreat in the mountains. We came around a corner and saw an older man hitchhiking between two mountain towns. Now I don't advocate picking up hitchhikers, but this had the signature of the Spirit on it from the start. We pulled over and asked him where he was headed. It turned out he was just going to the grocery store about fifteen miles ahead.

Over the next fifteen miles, we learned a lot about Wyatt. Before we ever opened our mouths, his appearance and aroma told us a lot about him. In recent history, he had lived on the streets. He was currently living in a barn in a town just west of the Colorado Front Range. By trade he was a sign maker, an artisan. He lit up when he talked about making signs. This was not a street person weaving a tale. You could see that it emerged from deep within him. He had fallen on hard times and had moved to the hills to live in the barn of some people he knew.

Why was Wyatt going to the store? Good question. A hotel and restaurant in the town, one of those places small towns are built around, was having its twentieth anniversary. There was a big shindig happening with food and drink for everyone in the town. And then we learned something more about Wyatt. When he heard that there was going to be a party, he decided to share another talent, another creative passion that bubbled up from within him. He wanted to cook and serve one of his favorite foods for the party—tamales! He was headed to a nearby town to pick up cornhusks for tamale shells, spending his all but depleted cash to serve the community celebration.

As we dropped Wyatt off at the store, I felt the Spirit's prompting, and moved to apply the lessons God was teaching me about affirming people. I said, "Wyatt, before you go, may I bless you? The God I serve tells me to bless people I meet."

He may have expected a financial blessing, but what he received did not seem to disappoint him. I prayed a brief prayer of blessing, identifying the divine image that I saw so clearly in this creation of God:

> *Father, thank You so much for Your creation, Wyatt. Thank You for reflecting Your image through him. Thank You for giving him the gift of creativity and his passion for sign making. Thank You for giving him a gift of hospitality and the desire to serve people through that gift, with his tamales. Father I can see You in him. Please reveal Yourself to him. Amen.*

Wyatt left the car with a smile on his face, walking a foot off the pavement. Someone had seen his worth, a majestic worth put there by the King. There it was again — the image of God leaking out from the cracks of one of His not-yet-redeemed creations.

Sometimes I feel that I shouldn't affirm non-believing people. Somehow in a warped kind of way, I think that if I affirm who they are, it will entrench them in their unredeemed state. I've come to believe that isn't true. There are innumerable opportunities for us to notice and affirm godly actions and the hint of God's image in our not-yet-rescued friends! Affirmations that identify God's fingerprints in their lives speak truth about God and allow us to bring a spiritual dimension to conversations.

TREASURE IN JARS OF CLAY

Helpful strategies and tactics notwithstanding, it's essential we recognize the amazing miracle at work in the spread of the good news of Christ. The early part of 2 Corinthians reveals ways the gospel moves forward through broken, surrendered, Spirit-led people. The apostle

Paul writes with such transparency, revealing his total dependence on Christ in the work of reaching unbelievers with the gospel.

> *The god of this age has blinded the minds of unbelievers, so that they cannot see the light of the gospel of the glory of Christ, who is the image of God. For we do not preach ourselves, but Jesus Christ as Lord, and ourselves as your servants for Jesus' sake. For God, who said, "Let light shine out of darkness," made his light shine in our hearts to give us the light of the knowledge of the glory of God in the face of Christ.*
>
> *But we have this treasure in jars of clay to show that this all-surpassing power is from God and not from us.* (4:4-7)

In the midst of a world filled with spiritually blind people, the gospel moves forward both through words and through service. Then we see that the same God who made light shine out of darkness (a reference to creation) has put His light in us. He defines that light as "the light of the knowledge of the glory of God." The same God who brought physical light to our world at the beginning, has now put a new light in the hearts of every believer. This light that is in us is the illumination of Jesus Christ. Before we open our mouths, do acts of service, or try to lead people to Jesus, we need to remember that the greatest resource we have available to us is the light of Jesus that resides in us. It is Jesus-light, embodied in weak, normal, everyday, broken human beings, which Paul refers to as "jars of clay."

Opportunities to let that light shine come often enough, if we are ready and willing. I've mentioned that one of the "third places" that Pam and I chose to make our own was a local Mexican food restaurant. Over the years, we got to know the owner, the managers, and a number of the wait staff. Our daughter even got a job there over summer break. We began to really know a number of our new friends there. One of the wait staff, John, took a liking to us. It seemed he was always giving us a little extra of our favorite appetizer or beverage.

We began requesting John's section, and we made sure that the evenings we went out to eat were the evenings on which John was working.

On a number of occasions, John would scoot into our booth and start talking with us. Periodically, John would ask what kind of work we were involved in. I would try to put it in terms he would understand: "I'm involved in the leadership of a non-profit. We equip leaders and everyday people—helping them grow in every area of life, including the spiritual dimension." That always seemed to satisfy him. We increasingly prayed for and tried to figure out how to move our friendship forward.

One night we heard all about his hopes to go back to college. He was in his late twenties and he told us once that he was "embarrassed that he hadn't grown up yet." We always tried to tip him a little extra as a message of support and encouragement. One night he came to our table all excited about just having come back from a trip to Las Vegas. A group of friends, some from the restaurant, had taken a wild trip together. He spared us the details, but he was happy to report that plenty of partying had gone on and he'd had a great time.

Soon after this encounter and after praying for the right timing, I asked John if he would join me for a bite to eat after he got off one of his afternoon shifts. He said "yes" and we put a date on our schedule. A week later we went out for appetizers and had a great time together. John asked me again what I did for work. I gave him a similar response as I had in the past, but this time he wanted to hear more.

"So is this some kind of Christian organization?" John asked.

"We help people develop as followers of Jesus, living out their faith with authenticity and genuineness," I replied.

From there we had a great conversation. John talked a bit about his own spiritual background and some of the things that had turned him off to "organized religion." Before we left the restaurant, I told John what a good time I had had. It was then that he said something to me that I will never forget: "Doug, I have a lot of regulars at the restaurant. I see a lot of people come through. You and your family are different. You care about people and you care about me. I look forward to the times you and Pam come in."

I hadn't talked in depth with John about spiritual things before that night. As we walk with God, the light of Jesus will shine out and people will see it even before we speak about it. John saw the difference Christ makes in a life because we loved him sincerely and took time to listen to him. The best thing we bring into any relationship with not-yet-believing people is the Spirit of God who dwells within us and has given us the treasure of eternal life.

LIVING REDEMPTIVELY

I hope this final part of our book has reshaped your understanding of evangelism. We have focused our discussion on how we can move more deeply into the lives of people yet to know Jesus Christ. We looked at positive motivations for sharing Christ with others— looking to Him as our model of how a sent one lives and speaks the message of grace. We viewed the breadth of the good news of Christ and how our understanding of its height, breadth, width, and depth can broaden our views of communicating it and living it out before our lost friends. We learned simple lessons to help us move into the worlds of those who don't know Christ, how to engage in the patient process of people moving toward Him, and ways to serve, affirm, and display Christ in ways that might deepen our relationships. While each of us should have the ability to articulate the message of Christ in simple, unreligious language, the spread of the gospel through our lives will be built upon the relationships we have with others right where we live, work, study, and play.

QUESTIONS FOR REFLECTION

- Are there people in your life who don't yet know Christ that you could serve intentionally this next week? Who are they and what can you do to serve them in love?
- Consider some of the non-believing people you are around on a regular basis. What can you see in their lives that shows, despite their sin, they were made in the image of God? Is there a way that you can affirm them or point out this character trait?

WAVES OF GRACE TOUCHING DISTANT SHORES

I looked and there before me was a great multitude that no one could count, from every nation, tribe, people and language, standing before the throne and in front of the Lamb.

— JOHN (REVELATION 7:9)

WE BEGAN OUR journey with the vision that God desires to use every person in the transmission of waves of grace. The ripple effect of God's grace in your life is meant to spread through you to a hungry and sin-sick world. Through the pages of this book, we have painted a picture of the kind of life God intends for you, and the kind of life you might reproduce in others around you, helping them to follow Jesus and be increasingly transformed into His likeness.

As we look back over the five parts of this book, let us consider how each of them work together to reflect God's purposes for us.

In part 1, "Crashing Waves," we learned that God deeply desires to heal and use the weak, the broken, the small, the unlikely, the imperfect, and the childlike. The kingdom of God is entered through the doorway of poverty, brokenness, and dependence. There is no other avenue to true spiritual life. The first three beatitudes of Jesus, found in the Sermon of the Mount, reflect this idea. It is the poor, mourning, and meek who are most blessed, embodying the kingdom of God.

Those first beatitudes also serve to point us in the direction of the fourth: "Blessed are those who hunger and thirst for righteousness, for they will be filled" (Matthew 5:6).

Part 2, "Streams of Fresh Water," helped us to consider the motivation, means, and result of a life pursuit of God. We long for God and follow Him through engagement in the Scriptures and faith-filled prayers that keep in mind His promises and faithfulness. And we saw that the outcome of our pursuit is a life that reflects Him.

Part 3, "The Coral Reef," reminded us that our pursuit of God is not a journey taken alone, but rather with others in the context of community. We saw the indispensible minimums for a community of Jesus and His kingdom. Our life with others is to manifest the markings of interdependence and authentic vulnerability. When that is true, our relationships will experience a love, freedom, and intimacy that lead to personal transformation. When a watching world sees these kinds of relationships, they will be drawn to Christ, naturally moving the mission of God forward. When we experience these first four aspects of community, we will be drawn into whole-life worship that exalts God through our words, actions, thoughts, and feelings. Community is a great accelerator of our own transformation, the spread of the gospel, and it increases the honor and glory given to God.

Part 4, "Na Pali Coast," revealed the outcome of our brokenness, our pursuit of God, and a community of friends on a spiritual journey: transformation. The Holy Spirit uses that threefold foundation to change us into men and women of faith, hope, and love, who increasingly reflect the life of Jesus to a watching world. God doesn't throw a whole life away just because it's banged up a little. He graciously molds and transforms our lives and creates in us a faith that brings His goodness to our helpless world.

Can you see why we finished with part 5, "Eternal Ripples"? If we live out the truths of parts 1–4, we experience what the world longs to have. When God's people live out of humble brokenness and dependence, when they long after God, when they join together in authentic community marked by vulnerable friendships and are actually changing and becoming more gentle spouses, Spirit-led parents, and honest employers, their friends and family will want what they have. Mission, the advance of the gospel, is the natural outflow of a life lived with Jesus and a few good friends.

So you see, broken dependence leads us to pursue God. Our pursuit of God, combined with the sharpening and molding of a community of friends, sets the stage for a Spirit-transformed life. The combination of all these is the most impressive and attractive audiovisual experience that our not-yet-believing friends can imagine. In appendix D I have included a picture that takes these principles for a life of following Jesus and portrays them visually in an illustration similar to the Navigator Wheel (see appendix C).

GOD CAN USE YOU

Who will God use for His purposes in our world? Anyone who is willing to come to Him and learn from Him. The one who seeks His purposes and walks in His ways is a candidate for a life of divine usefulness.

The accounts and stories throughout the Scripture communicate that God has a destiny and purpose for each of us. Some roles are small, some hidden from public sight, some spectacular. Some contributions are lived out among the many, others among the few. Some kingdom citizens live and minister among the powerful while others dwell among the powerless and oppressed. Each role, contribution, and location is significant because it has been chosen and ordained by the heavenly orchestra Conductor, the One who brings us together so that we each may provide our unique sounds, tones, and rhythms to His symphony.

At that first Christmas, when Jesus was born, look at who and what God chose to use for His earth-changing plan: a teenage unwed mother in a drafty manger in a dark corner of a remote suburb of Jerusalem. Not exactly the setting or cast for a drama of epic proportions! And then when Christ is born, no local celebrities arrive and no front-page story appears in the *Bethlehem Times*. No, the first worshippers, chosen specifically for the job, were sheep-stinky shepherds.

Do you get it? God is not about position, title, or pedigree. From the beginning of the Christ story to the adventure that continues in us to this day, God chose everyday people to play roles of significance in the story. Imagine the thoughts of that teenage girl, cradling the newborn King, as she "treasured up all these things and pondered them in her heart" (Luke 2:19). If God can use the fallible and stumbling heroes of the Old Testament, and if He introduces His Son to the world with a cast like this, He can use us.

Many years later, Jesus' good friend Peter wrote this compelling exhortation to a community of Christ followers much like us:

> But you are a chosen people, a royal priesthood, a holy nation, a people belonging to God, that you may declare the praises of him who called you out of darkness into his wonderful light. Once you were not a people, but now you are the people of God; once you had not received mercy, but now you have received mercy.
>
> Dear friends, I urge you, as aliens and strangers in the world, to abstain from sinful desires, which war against your soul. Live such good lives among the pagans that, though they accuse you of doing wrong, they may see your good deeds and glorify God on the day he visits us. (1 Peter 2:9-12)

These words were not written to scholars, politicians, supermodels, or superstar performers or athletes, though some may have been in the audience. These words were written to everyday people suffering in an imperfect world, showing up to work each day, going through the challenges of child-rearing and challenged by in-laws who didn't "get them." Yes, these everyday folks were filled with the Spirit of God and were drawn by the grace of God into a relationship with their risen Lord, Jesus. God can, longs to, and will touch you, change you, and use your life to send out powerful waves of grace through your family, neighborhood, and circle of friends.

EVEN TO DISTANT SHORES

During high school, at our local community pool, my friends and I would periodically get a twinkle in our eye and decide to "rock the pool." This amounted to five or six of us teenage guys repeatedly jumping off the high dive for fifteen minutes or so, creating tsunami-like waves that sent little kids running and middle-aged women grabbing their romance novels off the pool deck. Wave after wave came surging out of the pool and over its edges. We were probably the only ones really amused by this "rocking." Well, God intends to use us in such a way that our wave-making lives send swells to the end of the world.

You may remember that when we began our journey in chapter 1, I told the story of God giving me a promise verse that gave me a sense of destiny and clarity about His desire to use everyday people to bring generational impact through their lives. It was God's promise to Abraham:

> *I will surely bless you and make your descendants as numerous as the stars in the sky and as the sand on the seashore. Your descendants will take possession of the cities of their enemies, and through your offspring all nations on earth will be blessed, because you have obeyed me.* (Genesis 22:17-18)

You'll notice at the end of this short passage God promises to bless all the nations of the earth. While I didn't see or understand the implications of those words back during my college days, over the years I've come to realize that God's plans are to see waves of His grace cascade to the shores of every continent and every language and every people group.

Recognizing God's broad, world-embracing vision, my wife, Pam, and I have intentionally prayed and worked to join God in that purpose. We have worked to teach friends and family about God's heart and purposes for the whole world and to expose our children, our friends, and those we help spiritually to world missions. We've taken service trips across cultures within the United States, taken groups of high school and college students on mission trips to other countries, and we did a family trip to serve in the villages outside of Rio de Janeiro, Brazil. Over the years, we've seen God answer many of our prayers and fulfill His promises. We've seen God call and send young men and women to every continent of the world, bringing the good news of Christ with them, either through business, education, or mission involvement. When you begin to pass along the grace of God and the good news of Christ to others, discipling and mentoring other family members, neighbors, and friends into a deeper walk with Christ, you find that some of them cross cultures, thus fulfilling God's purposes.

The book of Revelation gives us a picture of the end of time. Notice carefully *who* will be attending that end of time worship service:

> *After this I looked and there before me was a great multitude that no one could count, from every nation, tribe, people and language, standing before the throne and in front of the Lamb. They were wearing white robes and were holding palm branches in their hands. And they cried out in a loud voice:*
>
> > *"Salvation belongs to our God,*
> > *who sits on the throne,*
> > *and to the Lamb."*

All the angels were standing around the throne and around the elders and the four living creatures. They fell down on their faces before the throne and worshiped God, saying:

"Amen!
Praise and glory
and wisdom and thanks and honor
and power and strength
be to our God for ever and ever.
Amen!" (7:9-12)

As you consider the influence of the grace of God on your life and the influence God's grace will have in your world—your family, friends, community, and country—keep in mind that God will even use us to bring His waves of grace to the ends of the earth.

THE WORD HAND

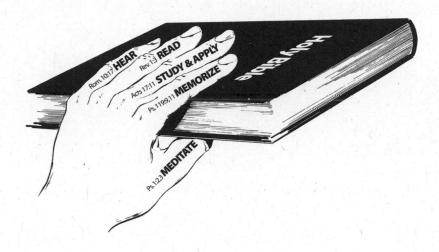

The "Word Hand" shows five very important methods of learning from the Bible.

HEARING
Romans 10:17
Hearing the Word from godly leaders and teachers provides insight into others' study of the Scriptures as well as stimulating your own appetite for the Word.

READING

Revelation 1:3

Reading the Bible gives an overall picture of God's Word. Many people find it helpful to use a daily reading program, which takes them systematically through the Bible.

STUDYING AND APPLYING

Acts 17:11

Studying and applying the Scriptures leads to personal discoveries of God's truths. Writing down these discoveries helps you organize and remember them.

MEMORIZING

Psalm 119:9,11

Memorizing God's Word enables use of the Sword of the Spirit to overcome Satan and temptations . . . to have it readily available for interactions with those yet to embrace Christ or helping other believers with a "word in season."

MEDITATING

Psalm 1:2-3

Meditation is the thumb of the Word Hand, for it is used in conjunction with each of the other methods. Only as you meditate on God's Word—thinking of its meaning and application in your life—will you discover its transforming power at work within you.

THE BRIDGE ILLUSTRATION

THE WHEEL
ILLUSTRATION

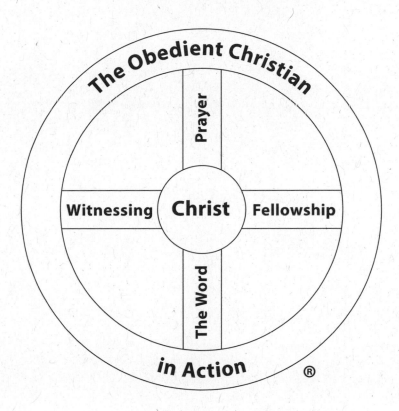

ESSENTIALS FOR WAVEMAKERS

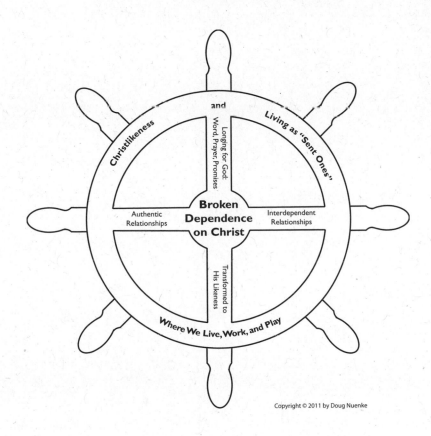

Christlikeness

and

Living as "Sent Ones"

Longing for God:
Word, Prayer, Promises

Authentic
Relationships

**Broken
Dependence
on Christ**

Interdependent
Relationships

Transformed to
His Likeness

Where We Live, Work, and Play

NOTES

INTRODUCTION: YOU, TOO, CAN MAKE SOME WAVES!

1. In the past twenty-five years, there has been a proliferation of writing by authors such as David Bosch, Darrell Guder, Lesslie Newbigin, Reggie McNeal, Michael Frost, and Alan Hirsch bringing clarity and correction to our mission and purpose as the body of Christ.
2. Michael Frost and Alan Hirsch, *The Shaping of Things to Come: Innovation and Mission for the 21st-Century Church* (Peabody, MA: Hendrickson, 2003), 19–21.
3. Eddie Gibbs, *LeadershipNext* (Downers Grove, IL: InterVarsity, 2005), 44.
4. Url Scaramanga, "Willow Creek Repents?" *Out of Ur Blog*, October 18, 2007, http://www.outofur.com/archives/2007/10/willow_creek_re.html.
5. John Eldredge, *Waking the Dead* (Nashville: Thomas Nelson, 2003), 75.

CHAPTER 1: BROKENNESS OPENS THE DOOR

1. D. Martyn Lloyd-Jones, *Studies in the Sermon on the Mount* (Grand Rapids, MI: Eerdmans, 1976), 33.
2. Calvin Miller, *Into the Depths of God* (Minneapolis: Bethany, 2000), 151.

CHAPTER 2: BEAUTY INSTEAD OF ASHES

1. John Fischer, "Losin' Is Winnin'," *Dark Horse* (Nashville: Word Music, 1982). Used by permission.

CHAPTER 3: THE LITTLE ONES GOD USES

1. Jean Vanier, *From Brokenness to Community* (Jahwah, NJ: Paulist, 1992), 26–27.

CHAPTER 4: WHERE GOSPEL SEED SPROUTS
1. John Fischer, "Beggar," *Dark Horse* (Nashville: Word Music, 1982). Used by permission.

CHAPTER 6: WHAT THE BIBLE IS NOT
1. James Montgomery Boice, *Foundations of the Christian Faith* (Downers Grove, IL: InterVarsity, 1986), 53–54.

CHAPTER 7: FINDING GOD IN PRAYER AND HIS PROMISES
1. J. I. Packer, *Knowing God* (Downers Grove, IL: InterVarsity, 1973), 103.
2. Tom Yeakley, *Praying Over God's Promises* (Tom Yeakley, 2007), 17.
3. J. O. Sanders, in Yeakley, 16–17.

CHAPTER 8: INTO HIS IMAGE
1. Anthony A. Hoekema, *Created in God's Image* (Grand Rapids, MI: Eerdmans, 1986), 67.
2. Walter Brueggemann, *Genesis* (Atlanta: John Knox, 1982), 31.
3. C. S. Lewis, *Mere Christianity* (New York: Macmillan, 1952), 153.

CHAPTER 9: COMMUNITY: GOD'S DESIGN FOR LIFE
1. Gilbert Bilezikian, *Community 101: Reclaiming the Local Church as Community of Oneness* (Grand Rapids, MI: Zondervan, 1997), 28–29.
2. Janet Kornblum, "Study: 25% of Americans Have No One to Confide In," *USA Today,* June 25, 2006.
3. Walter Brueggemann, *Genesis* (Atlanta: John Knox, 1982), 117.
4. J. I. Durham, *Exodus: Word Biblical Commentary* (Dallas: Word, 1987), 263.
5. Alexander Balmain Bruce, *The Training of the Twelve* (Grand Rapids, MI: Kregel, 1971), 12.
6. Tim Keller, "Community of Grace," sermon preached April 24, 2005, at Redeemer Presbyterian Church in New York City.
7. Peter H. Davids, *The First Epistle of Peter: The New International Commentary on the New Testament* (Grand Rapids, MI: Eerdmans, 1990), 86–87.

CHAPTER 10: LIVING IN INTERDEPENDENCE

1. Elton Trueblood, *The Yoke of Christ and Other Sermons* (New York: Harper, 1958), 25.
2. Gilbert G. Bilezikian, *Community 101: Reclaiming the Local Church as a Community of Oneness* (Grand Rapids, MI: Zondervan, 1997), 16.
3. Saint Augustine, *On Genesis* (Hyde Park, NY: New City, 2002), 234.
4. Dietrich Bonhoeffer, *Life Together* (New York: Harper, 1954), 21.
5. John Eldredge, *Waking the Dead* (Nashville: Thomas Nelson, 2006), 203.

CHAPTER 11: AUTHENTIC VULNERABILITY

1. M. McPherson, L. Smith-Lovin, and M. E. Brashears, "Social Isolation in America: Changes in Core Discussion Networks Over Two Decades," *American Sociological Review* 71, no. 3 (June 2006): 357–358.
2. Leadership Catalyst workshop, "Forming a High-Trust Culture."
3. Dietrich Bonhoeffer, *Life Together* (New York: Harper, 1954), 110.
4. John Ortberg, *Leadership Journal* 26, no. 3 (Summer 2005): 35.

CHAPTER 12: TRANSFORMING RELATIONSHIPS

1. John Ortberg, *The Me I Want to Be* (Grand Rapids, MI: Zondervan, 2010), 69.

CHAPTER 13: AN ETERNAL PURPOSE

1. David Jacobus Bosch, *Transforming Mission: Paradigm Shifts in Theology of Mission* (Maryknoll, NY: Orbis Books, 1991), 390.
2. Lesslie Newbigin, *The Household of God: Lectures on the Nature of the Church* (New York: Friendship Press, 1954), 163.
3. Craig Van Gelder, *The Essence of the Church* (Grand Rapids, MI: Baker, 2000), 125.
4. George Hunter, *The Celtic Way of Evangelism* (Nashville: Abingdon Press, 2000), 35.

CHAPTER 14: WHOLE-LIFE WORSHIP

1. Tim Keller, "Community of Grace," sermon preached April 24, 2005, at Redeemer Presbyterian Church in New York City.
2. Dallas Willard, *The Divine Conspiracy* (New York: HarperCollins, 1998), 364.
3. Jean Vanier, *Community and Growth*, rev. ed. (Bombay: St. Paul Publications, 1991), 55–58.

CHAPTER 15: LIFE IN THE GAP

1. Billy Graham, *The Holy Spirit* (Waco, TX: Word, 1978), 86.
2. *Seabiscuit*, directed by Gary Ross (Universal City, CA: Universal Pictures, 2003), http://www.imdb.com/title/tt0329575/quotes.
3. Andrew Murray, *Humility* (Minneapolis: Bethany, 2001), 56–57.
4. John Ortberg, *The Me I Want to Be* (Grand Rapids, MI: Zondervan, 2010), 38–39.

CHAPTER 17: SO YOU WANT TO BE LIKE JESUS

1. C. S. Lewis, *The Voyage of the Dawn Treader* (New York: Collier, 1976), 75.
2. Lewis, 90–91.

CHAPTER 18: THE SPIRIT OF GOD AND HIS SCALPEL

1. Jim Downing, "Meditation," The Navigators Singapore, 1983, 30.
2. Eugene Petersen, *Christ Plays in Ten Thousand Places* (Grand Rapids, MI: Eerdmans, 2005), 106–107.

CHAPTER 19: WHO DO YOU THINK YOU ARE?

1. Sid Huston's insights on his C.R.O.W.N. acrostic and teaching tool can be found in chapter 8 of his book, *The Little Pirate*. Sid Huston, *The Little Pirate* (Colorado Springs, CO: Mother's House Publishing, 2009), 60.

CHAPTER 20: TRANSFORMATION AS REVOLUTION

1. John Ortberg, *The Me I Want to Be* (Grand Rapids, MI: Zondervan, 2010), 51.
2. Steven Garber, *Fabric of Faithfulness* (Downers Grove, IL: InterVarsity, 2007), 56.
3. Walker Percy, *The Second Coming* (New York: Picador, 1980), 32.
4. Vernon Grounds, *Evangelicalism and Social Responsibility* (Scottdale, PA: Herald, 1972), 3.
5. In his sermon "Community of Grace," preached April 24, 2005, at Redeemer Presbyterian Church in New York City, Tim Keller spoke of the connection between Hebrews 12:28 and the beginning verses of chapter 13. He pointed out that the early manuscripts did not have chapter and verse numbering, so we are best to keep these sections together.

6. Rodney Clapp, *A Peculiar People* (Downers Grove, IL: InterVarsity, 1996), 199–200.
7. Bob Beltz and Walt Kallastad, *World Changers: Live to Serve* (Colorado Springs, CO: The Marriage CoMission, 2007), 42–43.
8. See http://en.wikipedia.org/wiki/Moravian_Church and http://www.ctlibrary.com/ch/1982/issue1/120.html.
9. Henri Nouwen, *The Selfless Way of Christ* (Maryknoll, NY: Orbis Books, 2009), 20.

CHAPTER 21: MOTIVATION FOR GOD'S MISSION

1. Doug Nuenke, *Latte Love* (Colorado Springs, CO: NavPress, 2011), 8.

ABOUT THE AUTHOR

DOUG NUENKE serves as U.S. president of The Navigators and leads with a fervor that comes from a continually growing relationship with God. Doug came to faith at Texas Christian University through the influence of a group of Christ-following friends. It was there he met his wife, Pam.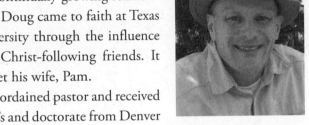

Doug is an ordained pastor and received both his master's and doctorate from Denver Seminary. His doctoral thesis was on the topic of biblical community and the spread of the gospel among men and women in their twenties and early thirties. He and Pam came on staff with The Navigators in 1992 initially to work with college students. Before taking the role of president, Doug led the Metro Mission, The Navigators' work in U.S. cities.

Doug and Pam now live in Colorado Springs and enjoy helping people walk with God and with one another. Doug loves to fly-fish, and he and Pam both appreciate spending time at their local coffee shop, hiking and the outdoors, reading, spending time with their three adult children, and meeting new friends in their community.

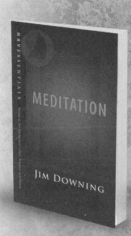

Support the Ministry
of The Navigators

The Navigators' calling is to advance the gospel of Jesus and
His kingdom into the nations through spiritual generations
of laborers living and discipling among the lost.

Navigators have invested their lives in people for more than 75 years,
coming alongside them life on life to help them passionately know
Christ and to make Him known.

The U.S. Navigators' ministry touches lives in varied settings, including
college campuses, military bases, downtown offices, urban neighborhoods,
prisons, and youth camps.

Dedicated to helping people navigate spiritually, The Navigators aims
to make a permanent difference in the lives of people around the
world. The Navigators helps its communities of friends to follow Christ
passionately and equip them effectively to go out and do the same.

To learn more about donating to The Navigators' ministry,
go to **www.navigators.org/us/support**
or call toll-free at **1-866-568-7827**.